Which? Way to Make Soft Furnishings

Jacqueline
Thompson
8/5/00 .

Which? Way to
Make Soft Furnishings

Consumers' Association
and Hodder & Stoughton

Which? Books are commissioned by The Association for Consumer Research and published by
Consumers' Association, 2 Marylebone Road, London NW1 4DX
and Hodder & Stoughton, 47 Bedford Square, London WC1B 3DP

Originally compiled by David Mason
Design and illustrations by Libra Studios, Twickenham, Middlesex

First published 1983
First reprint 1986
Second reprint 1987
Third reprint 1988
New edition September 1991

British Library Cataloguing in Publication Data
Mason, David
    Which? Way to Make Soft Furnishings
    1. Household soft furnishings. Making
    I. Title
    646.21
    ISBN 0-340-55006-6

Thanks for choosing this book . . .

If you find it useful, we'd like to hear from you. Even if it doesn't live up to your
expectations or do the job you were expecting, we'd still like to know. Then
we can take your comments into account when preparing similar titles or,
indeed, the next edition of the book. Address your letter to: Publishing
Manager, Consumers' Association, FREEPOST, 2 Marylebone Road, London
NW1 4DX. We look forward to hearing from you.

Typeset by Tradespools, Frome, Somerset
Printed and bound in Great Britain by Jolly & Barber, Rugby, Warwickshire

Contents

Conversion chart

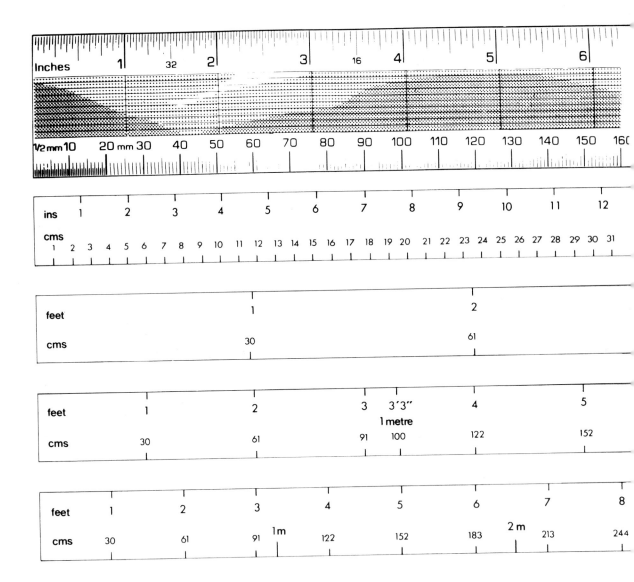

Introduction

Making soft furnishings is a craft and, as with all crafts, it is the individual character of an article that gives it quality and value. Few professionals can spare the time that such individuality needs if they are to make an adequate living, but someone at home can afford to take greater care and invest more effort in order to create a beautiful object. This book demonstrates that it is not beyond the scope of most people's skills to make soft-furnished articles which match the best available in terms of professional workmanship, but which also carry the individual mark of the person who made them.

We have included a spectrum of projects ranging in size from bed hangings to a simple tea cosy. The large items are not invariably the most difficult – some of the curtains and bedspreads are quite straightforward – and the small items not always quick and easy, particularly if they involve extra decorative stages. But, in general, many of the projects are much easier than they might appear. Table linen and cushions are among the most rewarding items, particularly for sewing novices, since they are open to the most individual approaches without requiring too great an outlay of either time or money.

In soft furnishing a great deal of material can be involved, but even so it is wise to spend as much as you can afford since good quality will pay off in longevity and continuing good looks. One of the main advantages of doing the work yourself is that it may allow you to choose a better quality extravagant fabric.

The skills required are relatively basic – the standard stitches and techniques are explained at the beginning of the book.

Don't tackle soft furnishing in a confined space. A large expanse of floor is probably one of the most useful things to have, second only to a sewing-machine. As with dressmaking, it is best to have the ironing-board up all the time while you work so that there is no temptation *not* to press seams as you go along. Assemble all the tools and equipment before you start so that you don't suddenly realise that you lack something absolutely vital just as you come to a tricky bit.

Special techniques such as piping edges, lock-stitching linings to curtains and lampshade-making are described where they are immediately relevant. Similarly, those that fit more into the realms of upholstery are explained in context. If you become lured by the idea of upholstery, see this book's companion volume, *Which? Way to Repair and Restore Furniture*.

Other cardinal rules for a professional-looking article: plan your scheme and allow a lot of time for wandering round furniture shops and fabric departments as well as browsing through magazines; don't skimp at the measuring stages; and when you do start cutting, fitting and sewing, allow enough time for each session so that you can enjoy the sense of accomplishment that makes soft furnishing such a satisfying and creative occupation.

1 Basic sewing techniques

The sewing skills required in soft furnishing are few. Anyone with a basic grounding in sewing should be able to master them, and someone who has tackled the far more intricate work of dressmaking will find soft furnishing relatively easy.

STITCHES

Tacking
This is a quick temporary stitch for holding together two or more pieces of fabric before the final stitching is put in, but can often be omitted if the fitting and pinning stages are carefully done.

Cut a short length of thread (40–50cm), too much becomes easily knotted, and make a small backstitch at the start of the line for tacking. Sew through both or all pieces of fabric, along the line where the final stitching is to be. Push the needle down through the fabric and back towards you in a single movement, forming stitches about a centimetre long. Pull the needle back out of the fabric until the thread is taut, but don't pull the fabric out of shape.

At the end, sew a couple of times through the fabric and cut the thread. When you have completed your final sewing you can cut the tacking at any point and pull it out leaving no trace.

An alternative to this is the quicker *uneven tacking*, particularly useful in curtain-making where large expanses of material are being dealt with. For the first stitch, take the needle along 2cm, form a stitch about 5mm long, then move along another 2cm to repeat the stitch.

Running (gathering) stitch
Often used for preparing material which is to be gathered up. Usually two parallel rows are made, 2mm apart, for strength. Work on either side of the fabric. Start with a knot or backstitch and weave the needle in and out of the fabric several times before pulling it through [1.1].

Backstitch
This is the hand-sewn equivalent of machine-stitching. In soft furnishing it is used for sewing zips into loose covers as it is very strong. It is also useful when the machine cannot cope with too many layers of material. Start with a small knot or double stitch. Sew through from front to back and along 5mm, bringing the needle through to the front, all in one movement. Pull the needle through to tighten the thread. Go back 2.5mm. Push the needle through to the back and along another 5mm. You will find that you are sewing a continuous line on both the front and back of the fabric [1.2].

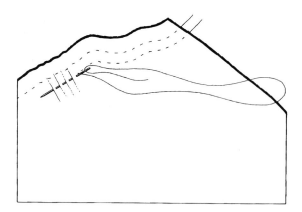

1.1   Running (gathering) stitch

1.2   Backstitch

1.3a and b Slip stitch

Slip stitch

This stitch is used extensively in sewing the side and bottom hems of curtains, and in other situations where the aim is to achieve neat stitching with hardly any marks showing on the facing side of the fabric. It is also used to join two folds of fabric, as in mitred corners (page 13).

To join a folded edge to a flat piece of material, as in a hem, have the fabric wrong side up, with the pinned or tacked hem ready for sewing towards you. Hold the beginning of the hem under your thumb and second finger, anchored underneath by your third finger. Start by making a small knot or two small stitches in the hem turning. Bring the needle out through the fold of the hem, and pick up two strands of the facing fabric on its wrong side [**1.3a and b**]. Do this carefully and neatly because it will show as a small point on the facing side when the article is finished. The points should be small and evenly spaced. Insert the needle into the hem exactly opposite the stitch, and run it along inside the hem for about 1cm. In the same movement, bring the needle out through the edge of the hem and pull the stitch taut but not tight. Repeat the sequence. On the facing side of the fabric you will see nothing more than a neat line of points.

When joining two folds of fabric, as in a mitred corner, insert the needle into the fold at the point exactly opposite, then let it emerge about 6 or 7mm along.

Hem stitch

This serves the same purpose as slip stitching when a fold is to be joined to a flat area of fabric and can be as nearly invisible on the right side if carefully done. It is not so neat as slip stitch on the wrong side but it is probably a little easier. Secure the thread at the beginning of the hem. Pick up a couple of threads from the wrong side of the flat piece of fabric, and in the same movement pick up a small amount through both layers of the hem. The needle should point diagonally as in the drawing. Pull the needle through to draw up the thread [**1.4**].

1.4 Hem stitch

1.5   Prepare a flat seam by pinning and tacking

1.6a and b Sew the seam, then overcast the seam allowances, either individually or together

SEAMS

Simple flat seam

This seam, used for joining fabric widths, consists of a single line of sewing far enough from the edges to avoid fraying. Pin the two fabrics edge to edge, right sides together [**1.5**]. If you like, tack along a line about 1.5cm from the edges, then sew along the same line, securing the seam ends with a couple of backstitches. Open out the fabric, wrong sides up. Separate the seam turnings and press them flat, unless there are instructions to the contrary [**1.6a and b**].

It is wise to neaten a simple seam to prevent the raw edges fraying. You can do this by following the method on page 39 (best if one of the pieces of fabric is gathered), or by overcasting or pinking.

To overcast work by bringing the needle through from behind the work at quite an acute angle. You can sew the two halves of the seam individually, or together if there won't be a problem of bulk. To overcast by ordinary sewing-machine, use zigzag stitch right on the edge of the trimmed seam allowance.

To pink the edges machine-sew along each seam-half 5mm from the raw edges, before cutting along with pinking shears [**1.7a and b**].

Grading seams

The purpose of this is to help a simple seam to lie as flat as possible when two or more pieces of fabric are joined together and need to lie to one side. It isn't necessary if you can open the seam out. The technique is often used when piping is involved. Each piece of fabric is trimmed to a slightly different width and then the longest one is pressed down over all of them to achieve a neat finish [**1.8**].

French seam

This seam encloses the raw edges within itself, avoiding the problems of fraying. It can be used, for example, on net curtains or unlined curtains but it is too bulky for heavy fabrics.

Place the pieces edge to edge, wrong sides together. Pin and sew along the length 1cm in from the edges, securing the ends of the thread with a couple of backstitches [**1.9a**]. Trim the seam allowance to 5mm. Turn the fabrics right

1.7a and b Machine along each individual seam allowance then trim the edges with pinking shears

1.8 Grading seams

1.9a, b and c French seam: [a] Sew the first seam, wrong sides together. [b] Fold back and press. [c] Sew the second seam, right sides together

sides together, and adjust them so that the sewing line is right on the edge. It may help to press the seam [**1.9b**]. Sew a second line exactly 1cm from the new edge [**1.9c**]. Open out the fabric. You will have a narrow tube standing out from the wrong side of the fabric. The double line of stitching gives additional strength to the seam. Press the tube down to one side.

1.10a and b   Run-and-fell seam: [a] Cut one seam allowance to half width. [b] Fold and press the wider side over the trimmed half

1.11a and b   Clipped curves and corners

Run-and-fell seam

This seam secures the tube to the wrong side of the curtain. It is useful for nets or other transparent fabrics where seams can be seen from the right side, and is also very strong with well-enclosed raw edges. Pin the two pieces right sides together. Sew along a line 1.5cm from the edge. Press the turnings to one side. Then trim the lower one to 7.5mm width [1.10a]. Fold the longer turning over the shorter one, tuck the edge under and press it to a neat line [1.10b]. Sew it to the wrong side of the curtain along its length. You could machine-sew it but if you don't want the seam to show, it is best to slip stitch the allowance to the fabric.

Clipping curves and corners

Clipping curves is done to enable fabric to lie flat when the stitching would otherwise pull it out of shape. Gentle curves do not need as many notches as sharp ones. Clipping corners helps to reduce bulk when the corner is turned to the inside [1.11a and b].

1.12a, b, c and d Mitring corners: [a] Press the corner. [b] Open out the folds. [c] Turn up the corner and trim. [d] Refold and slip stitch the diagonal

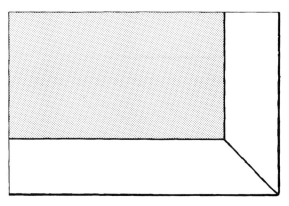

Mitring corners

Mitring is a method of neatening a corner, commonly used in the making of curtains and bedspreads. Turn in the raw edges at the corner by 5mm and press them. Then turn the edges over again so that these new folds are where you want the edge of the hem to be. Press them lightly [**1.12a**]. Open out the last folds and turn up the corner [**1.12b**]. Trim across the corner to 5mm [**1.12c**]. Then fold back the double hem with the two diagonal edges abutting neatly, and slip stitch them together [**1.12d**].

QUILTING

Quilting is one of the oldest of household crafts. It probably originated in Europe in the eleventh and twelfth centuries, with different regions developing their own traditional patterns. In its simplest form, it is a method of holding two layers of fabric together with a layer of insulation between them for warmth. Originally, almost any form of filling was used, from wool left by sheep on hedgerows to shreds of old material.

When making a quilted object, choose the simplest design to show off the work to best effect. Examples look well on cushions or throw-over bedspreads.

English quilting It is usual to use synthetic wadding as the filling, though 'bump' and 'domett' (flannel-like fabric of wool and cotton) are possible choices, or even an old blanket. Wadding is available in several thicknesses.

Natural fibres are the best for quilting. Man-made fibres are more resistant to shaping. Fabrics with a sheen, such as satin, show off patterns well. Velvet and fine wool also produce luxurious items. Backing consists of calico, muslin, sheeting, or the main fabric itself so that the quilt is reversible. A matt fabric is best for the underside of a bedcover, to prevent it slipping off the bed.

If machine-sewing the design, the stitches will go through all layers without difficulty. However, with a large bedcover, you will almost certainly be unable to get the work under the machine arm, necessitating either working by hand or dealing with the quilt in sections, making the final joins part of the overall design.

It is not necessary to cover the whole area with an elaborate design – you could work just the central part or even one corner. The remainder could be quilted with a simple all-over pattern of squared, rectangular or diamond stitches.

Cut out the fabric for the top and the backing. Add 7.5cm to the length and width to give 2.5cm turnings all round and to allow for the slight reduction in size caused by the quilting process.

Cut the wadding to the same size as the outer fabrics: if you have to join widths, overlap the edges of the wadding and secure them with a large running stitch.

Plan the design, deciding, if necessary, where the separate sections will join, so that the seams

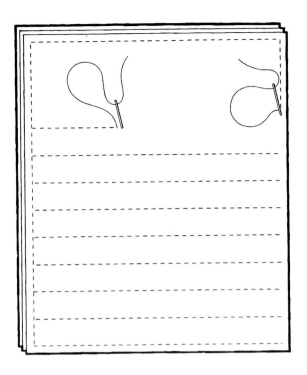

1.13   Prepare for quilting by tacking wadding and fabric together

1.14   Roll up spare quilt under the machine arm

can form part of the pattern. Sketch or trace the design on to tracing paper, and tack along the lines of the pattern. Tear away the tracing paper, leaving the design in tacking on the top fabric.

Alternatively, you could trace a design on the top layer using dressmaker's carbon paper. If you want to copy an interesting pattern taken from a book, cut a template in cardboard and draw round it with tailor's chalk.

Place the three layers of fabric together, with the wadding in the middle. Run a line of tacking stitches from side to side across the centre of the article and other lines parallel to it every 5cm or so, covering the whole quilt, and also tack round the edges. This will prevent the work from slipping about and causing puckering [1.13].

With the whole assembly fixed in place, you can start working on the design itself. Work from the centre outwards, sewing along your tacking or carbon paper markings. Keep the work as level and as even as possible to avoid puckering. Sew either by hand with an even running stitch or backstitch, or by machine if you can get the work under the machine arm [1.14]. If you are working a small item by hand, you can get the best results using an embroidery frame. When you have worked all round the design, sew the fixing stitches over the rest of the area. If you are machine-stitching, use a gauge to ensure that the sewing lines are accurately spaced.

If you have been working in sections, now is the time to join them together. Trim any excess fabric to within about 5mm of the finished dimensions. Fold in the turnings of one section by 5mm, and trim away the wadding so that it is level with the turned-in edges. Trim the wadding on the next section to the same level but do not fold in the turnings. Instead, place them between the folded edges of the first section so that the two pieces of wadding abut [1.15a and b]. Tack through all the layers and then topstitch along the edge of the folds.

To finish the outer edges, turn the two pieces of fabric in towards each other and secure them with a line of running stitches all round. A second line of stitches half a centimetre in from the edge will help to strengthen the hem [1.16a]. Alternatively, you can insert a length of piping or frill between the two outer fabrics. A third method is to bind the edges with a length of matching or contrasting fabric. Press in the edges of the binding, fold the fabric in two lengthwise, and sew it on all round the outside with a double line of stitches for security [1.16b].

Remove the tacking stitches from the quilting. The work should now show up the intended pattern in a form of low relief.

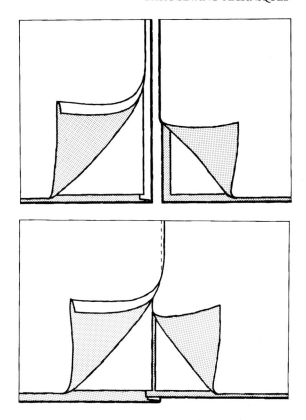

1.15a and b Finish the outer edges by [a] trimming wading and abutting edges, then [b] top stitching through all the layers

1.16a and b Finish the outer edges by [a] turning in, or [b] binding

1.17   Italian quilting

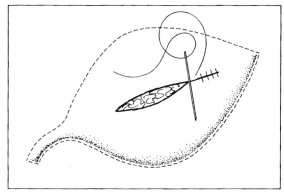

1.18   Trapunto quilting

Italian quilting Purely decorative and does not provide an extra layer of warmth since it has no inner wadding. Two rows of parallel stitching about 5mm apart are made round the design – often leaves, flowers or scrolls. These form a casing through which thick yarn or quilting wool is threaded to produce a raised effect. It is usual to use a fabric with a sheen which enhances the way the fabric rises and falls, but you can also work with transparent fabrics, such as georgette and jap silk, and thread different coloured silks through the casings (this is known as *shadow quilting*). You will need backing fabric, probably muslin or calico.

As with English quilting, transfer your design on to the right side of the main fabric, using tracing paper and tacking stitches, or dressmaker's carbon paper. The finished design will look the most attractive if it is not too dense or complex. Tack the two fabrics together with parallel lines of stitching the length of the material, and tack all round the edges. Hand-sew two parallel lines of stitching round the design using running stitch or backstitch; machine-stitching would be a perfectly feasible alternative. Thread a bodkin or blunt tapestry needle with quilting wool and from the back of the work introduce it into one of the channels between the muslin and the top fabric. Where you come to a sharp corner or curve bring the needle out again, always at the back of the work, and reintroduce it at the new angle through the same hole, so that there is a continuous raised line. Leave a small loop of wool at such places. This prevents the work from puckering [1.17].

Trapunto quilting Really a cross between English and Italian quilting in that single lines of stitching are made round the design, and then wadding is stuffed between the two layers of fabric to make large raised areas. You can use kapok, cotton wool or synthetic fibre as the padding.

Follow the same order for the other types of quilting: transfer the design on to the main fabric, tack the muslin and the main fabric together with rows of parallel stitching the length of the work and all round the edge; then sew round the design by machine or by hand using running stitch or backstitch.

Carefully slit the muslin in the centre of the area to be padded, feed in the filling with a bodkin or blunt needle so that you can ease it into any corners, and close up the slit [1.18].

PATCHWORK

Patchwork is often used as the basis for quilting. Patchwork developed not least as an economy measure for using up scraps of fabric, but its homely charm led to its development into a stylish craft. Used in conjunction with quilting, the patterns made by the arrangement of patches can be the basis of sewing lines so that each patch has a contoured shape. This helps to show up the selection of both pattern and fabric.

In some areas, especially North America, patchwork quilting became something of a social activity, particularly at quilting 'bees' where women gathered to practise their craft. Designs unique to certain regions evolved.

Before embarking on anything elaborate, it is best to start with a simple pattern of squares, rectangles or hexagons – the hexagon being the simplest with the least acute angles.

You can get metal and plastic master shapes or templates from craft shops and department stores [1.19]. Or make your own from stout card, measured and cut with extreme accuracy. Window templates are useful for placing over a patterned fabric to mask off the exact area that will show. The outer edge of the window template is the edge of the seam allowance.

The character of the patchwork will depend to a large extent on the fabrics you choose and the way you arrange the different colours and textures. It is best to use fabrics of a similar weight, and to avoid stretchy or easily frayed ones. If you plan to wash the quilt, remember to keep to washable and colourfast materials.

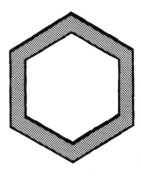

1.19 Patchwork templates, including a window template

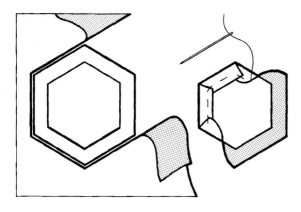

1.20a and b [a] Pin the paper to the fabric and cut round with 1cm allowance, then [b] fold over and tack the edges

1.21a and b Join the patches: [a] by overstitching, or [b] with herringbone stitch

Using the template, cut a number of pieces of paper (colour magazines are an excellent source and the ideal weight) to the exact size and shape required. Take one paper per patch and pin it to the wrong side of the fabric. Cut out the patch with a 1cm turning allowance all round [**1.20a**]. Turn the edges over the edge of the paper and tack through both fabric and paper, pleating the corners neatly as you go [**1.20b**]. Remove the pin. When you have several patches prepared (for example, seven patches are needed to make up a floret of hexagons), begin to join them together.

Place two patches right sides together and oversew with small, even stitches along one side only [**1.21a**]. Pick up the next patch and carry on in the same way. You will find that you can go along two or three sides without having to break off your thread, maybe more, although too long a thread will slow you down by getting caught up or knotted. Remember that the stitches should hardly show from the right side of the work, so each overstitch must pick up only a few threads from the edge of either patch. Pay special attention to the stitching at each corner; do not pull so tightly that you pucker the work, at the same time you should avoid gaping holes or any misalignment.

It is easiest to make up blocks of patches and then join the blocks to form the overall design. Press the work on the wrong *and* right sides but be sure to keep the papers in place to prevent the turnings leaving ridges on the right side. Finally, remove the papers by pulling out the tacking.

A more fancy effect is achieved by joining the patches with herringbone stitch [**1.21b**] if you do not intend actually quilting the work as a finishing touch.

If you have used a hexagonal or other non-right-angled shape, you may have to sew a set of several half-shapes in order to end up with a straight edge. You could then enclose the edge in a border as described for quilted work. Alternatively, you could mount the work on a plain fabric and then deal with the edges in the same way, or go on to work the patchwork into a quilt.

2   Curtains and blinds

Few skills are more valuable in your home than the ability to make your own curtains. Almost every room needs them, and they have a critical influence on its appearance. In general, a window's position and proportions in relation to the whole room can be enhanced or disguised appropriately.

If you choose a fabric which is in harmony with the other decorations and furnishings in the room, the curtains will have a calming influence. You might even consider having wallpaper and curtain fabric matching other items in the room. Or, for a dramatic effect, choose a fabric with a bold design (though large patterns are uneconomical because you will have to buy extra in order to match up the pattern).

The type of fabric itself can have a great influence on the character and style of a room. The subtle light-and-shade effect of plain velvet can generate a feeling of opulence. A colourful cotton print will cheer up an otherwise dingy space.

When choosing the fabric bear in mind that it may need to be hard-wearing and easy to clean. Towelling and plastic-coated fabrics would be practical choices for a kitchen or bathroom.

Some upholstery fabrics are too heavy and don't drape well, and even those heavy fabrics that *are* suitable (furnishing velvet, for instance) might have to be rejected if their bulk will cut down light when they are drawn back. If the room is quite dark, don't cut out more light than you need. If there is a radiator beneath the window, floor-length curtains may prevent the heat coming into the room efficiently when they are closed.

Most curtains benefit from being lined. The lining helps to keep the curtain clean, acts as an insulator against the cold and noise, looks neater from the outside of the house than the reverse side of the curtain fabric, and helps to stop the curtain fabric fading by taking the full impact of any direct sunlight (silk rots in sunlight). Choose lining fabric either to match the curtain fabric, or

in white, beige or cream. Coloured linings will show fading before pale ones, and may show through and affect the look of the curtain adversely.

You can also add interlining. Lined-and-interlined curtains are only slightly more difficult to make than lined-only curtains, and are worth the extra expense. The interlining is a layer of cotton-based or synthetic fabric between the lining and the curtain. Correctly fitted, it gives the edges of the curtain a thickness and 'roll' that lends a touch of luxury to even the most modest fabrics and, perhaps more importantly, it forms an even more effective insulation barrier by keeping the heat inside and cutting out draughts. Make sure that the curtain fabric, lining and interlining are all compatible in terms of washing or dry-cleaning.

TRACKS AND FITTINGS

There is a bewildering array of curtain track fittings and hanging systems, and manufacturers change their ranges often. So the best way to choose is to study the range of tracks currently available.

Your choice will depend on your decorating scheme, on the type of heading and on the weight of the fabric. These will dictate the style and material of the track: it might be aluminium, plastic, brass, brass-plated metal, or wood. You might prefer a pole which would look elegant in some period settings, especially when used to carry full-length curtains in a large room. If you prefer the convenience of a track but the appearance of a pole, there is available a half-section pole which conceals a track mechanism.

If you are using a pelmet, a board will probably be essential to carry the weight (page 31), but a valance can be carried on a curtain track.

Tracks are available that can be bent to follow the contours of the area, such as a bay or dormer window. For a dormer window, a continuation of the track round the sides allows you to draw the

2.1 A track extending round the sides of a dormer window

curtain completely away from the window in order to let in as much light as possible [**2.1**].

If you prefer detachable linings, you may find it useful to install the type of track which takes a special kind of hooked glider on which you can hang both the curtain and the lining.

Most manufacturers make a system for opening and closing the curtains with a single pulled cord which will save the fabric from handling. You should also consider this if the curtains are very tall or heavy. It is possible to install an electrically operated opening-and-closing system.

If you are to close and open the curtains by hand, you can fit rods to the inner edge hooks to avoid handling and possibly soiling the curtain fabric itself. Or you can fit a tasselled draw-cord.

Heading tape

You will need to decide exactly which type of heading tape you want to use, and calculate the length. It is possible to make your own headings but there are enough good manufactured tapes for this to be unnecessary. If you are planning to make several curtains with the same heading, you might feel it worth investing in a full roll of the particular tape.

The main types of heading tapes in general use are as follows:

Standard tape Draws the curtain up into a simple gather. It produces a shallow heading and can be used with an exposed track but is generally more suitable for use with pelmets. It takes standard curtain hooks, which should be inserted every 8cm for medium-weight curtains. You will need twice the track width of both tape and fabric [**2.2a**].

Pencil pleat tape The most straightforward and satisfactory type of decorative tape when there is no pelmet. It draws up into a tidy series of tight pleats approximately the thickness of a pencil, and takes standard hooks. Some versions are stiffened to give a firm crisp heading, and an extra deep version (14cm) is available to give a well-proportioned heading for floor-length curtains. Special versions of pencil pleating tape are available for net and sheer curtains. Use 2½ times the track width for the deeper heading tape, and up to three times the track width for net curtains [**2.2b**].

Triple pleat tape Gives the effect of a group of three pinched pleats without the need for long-pronged hooks. Drawing up the strings produces spaced triple pleats. It is available in a variety of depths – 14cm, 9cm and 4cm – buy any of these to twice the track width [**2.2c**].

Cartridge pleat tape This heading produces a well-rolled pleat effect and evenly hanging curtains below the heading. Use the hooks recommended by the manufacturer. You will need twice the track width.

Lining tape Used for detachable linings and is hung on the curtain hooks [**2.12**].

Net heading tapes A wide range is available to give approximately the same choice of heading styles as on curtains: pencil pleats, plain gathers, pinch and triple pleats, and cylindrical pleats like the cartridge pleat.

Other equipment

Like good clothes, curtains look infinitely better if they are sewn by hand, and indeed all the hems on the curtains described here are hand-sewn, but a sewing-machine is necessary for applying the heading to the curtains, taking up the hems on the linings, joining widths of fabric, and other otherwise tedious jobs. (There are also iron-on materials available for turning up hems etc. without sewing.)

You will need pins, needles, synthetic sewing thread in a colour to match the curtain fabric, and enough hooks to fit the rings appropriate to the

2.2a, b and c [a] Standard heading. [b] Pencil pleat tape. [c] Triple pleat tape

located) plastic handles are light and quick to use, and unlikely to make your thumb joint ache. The advantage of the heavy steel scissors that tailors use is that you can sharpen them yourself.

An iron and ironing-board, and a fabric tape measure are also necessary. You will find the job of making hems and seams easier if you have a short ruler.

Measuring the window
The first job is to measure up for the curtains. Take a notebook and pencil to the window, together with a rule and a chair or stepladder for standing on. A metre stick or an extending steel rule is useful. (All measurements here are metric, but there is a conversion chart on page 6.)

Sketch a picture of the window on your note-pad and determine how far on each side, and above and below, the curtain should extend. First the height above, which will be where the track will fit. If the window is extremely small, 8cm will be sufficient. If the window is slightly larger, say one metre or more in depth, then a distance of 12cm will be approximately right for the position of the track.

Determine the finished width of the track. Remember that if the window is wide you will need more space at each side for containing the curtain when it is drawn back. If you have chosen to fit the track 12cm above the window, then a distance of 12cm on each side will be appropriate. If the window is smaller, and the track lower, it should extend less at the sides.

Lastly, work out the length of the curtain. Put a small pencil mark on the wall below the sill at the point where you think the bottom of the curtain should hang. Again, 12cm or a little more below the window will be about right. If the curtains are to hang in a recess, let them fall to about 1cm above the recess. Floor-length curtains should hang about 1 cm above the floor.

Fitting the track
Now fit your track following the manufacturer's instructions. Hang a track ring or glider in the appropriate groove and measure from the bottom of the ring down to the mark on the wall showing the bottom of the curtain. This is known as the 'hook drop'. You will need to make sure this measurement is absolutely accurate.

length of track – your supplier will tell you what you need. If you haven't already got a pair of scissors, it is worth investing in the best pair of dressmaking scissors you can afford (this applies to any of the projects in this book). Modern scissors in a lightweight alloy with coloured (and easily

2.3 A half-repeat doesn't look so obvious at the top, when it will be obscured in the heading

THE FABRIC

Now you can calculate the width of material to buy. Generally, you should aim for a width of material to be twice the length of the track. When the curtains are closed, they will then fall into neat folds. If you have less than this double width, the curtains will look flat and skimped. If you have more, they may not hang comfortably when drawn back off the window.

For a small window you need to have only one width of material in each curtain. So, assuming the track is 120cm wide, that is the width of material to choose (material is available in other widths). If your window is very narrow, say only 50 or 60cm, it would be better to use only one small curtain to cover it, hung to one side and using the widest fabric available. If it is over about 60cm, choose the narrower width of fabric, and make one curtain for each side of the window.

You can now calculate the length required. Recall your hook drop measurement. You will have to add two other measurements. One is for a hem at the bottom of the curtain: a double hem is recommended, so add 12cm. The other is for the heading at the top. This is the most interesting part of the curtain. It is structurally important because it carries the hooks that hold up the curtain, it covers the track when the curtains are closed, and it is also an important part of the decoration. For this small curtain a simple pencil pleat will be appropriate. To form this type of

heading, you should add 7.5cm to the length. Add a further 15cm to the total length so that you can square off the material in case it is cut badly in the shop.

So the formula (in centimetres) for working out the amount of material to buy for a simple pair of curtains with no widths joined is:

Hook drop (*say*)   210
               +12   (*hem*)
               + 7.5(*heading**)

      =   229.5
           × 2   (*for 2 curtains*)

      =   459
           +15   (*to offset shop's possible bad cutting*)

Total =   474   (*cm*)

**This is for pencil pleats – other heading tapes may need more or less.*

Round the total up to the nearest quarter of a metre or other amount that the shop is willing to sell you.

If necessary, add the length of the pattern repeat to your calculations for each curtain, since you will have to cut the two pieces to match. Bear in mind that the bottom of the repeat should occur at the foot of the curtains (after the hem is taken up).

If you have to join widths because a single width won't be enough, consider the material you are using. As a general rule, light curtains need a greater width than heavy ones. Also, take into account the heading you have chosen: simple gathered headings need about 1½ times the width of the track, pinch pleats need 2–2½ times that width, and pencil pleats and various other headings up to three times the width of the track. It is a false economy to skimp on the fullness as the curtains will look wrong.

If the curtains are to overlap in the middle when drawn, add on 15cm to each curtain's width. Add a further 5cm for each side hem (20cm in total). This will give you the total width of curtaining. Divide that total by the width of the fabric on the roll, and round the answer up to the next whole figure: this is the total number of widths you will need.

In order to arrive at the amount of material to buy, multiply the total length of the curtain (including hem and heading but not allowing extra at this stage for a possible cutting error in the shop) by the total number of widths needed. Add on the depth of any pattern repeat multiplied by the total number of widths, and round up the figure to the next half-metre to allow for cutting errors in the shop and for shrinkage.

Your total requirements will be increased if you plan to make a pelmet, valance and/or fabric tie-backs. See pages 34 and 40 for guidance on how to work out your extra requirements.

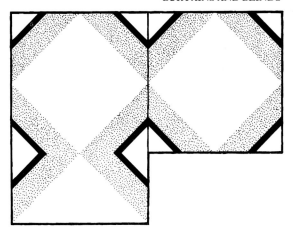

2.4   Join widths symmetrically

Cutting the fabric

Spread out the fabric on the table or floor. First you need to establish a straight line across one end, at right angles to the selvedges. All the lengths of fabric must be cut from this line – otherwise the curtains will not hang properly. The preferred way is to pull a thread from across the weave if it is a fairly loose-woven fabric. If the fabric is printed linen or chintz you are unlikely to be able to do this as the grain tends to shift during the printing process, so line the fabric up with the end of the table to give you a right angle, or use a set square.

If the fabric is patterned, the curtains will look best if the pattern repeat coincides with the bottom of the curtain after the hem has been taken up. A half-repeat doesn't look so obvious at the top of the curtain where it will be obscured in the heading [2.3]. So cut the lengths of fabric starting 12cm (the total amount needed to form the hem) below the bottom of a repeat.

As with all soft furnishing, it is wise to follow the maxim 'measure twice, cut once'. Refer to the measurements list and mark off the cutting points with a couple of pins. Check that the measurements still hold good before you cut. As you cut off each length, mark what will be the top with dressmaker's chalk, pins or a tacking stitch. This is especially important for a fabric with a pile or nap, such as velvet, when all the pieces must run in the same direction – if the pile runs downwards you can dust the curtains more easily but they will look more opulent if the pile runs upwards.

2.5   Selvedges snipped to release any tension in the join

Joining widths of fabric

If you have to join widths, lay out the pieces in front of the window to make sure that you get all the parts in the right places. Join the widths symmetrically [2.4]. It looks better if you arrange the seams to fall towards the outer edges of the curtain.

When you have laid out the pieces, snip off a small triangle from the corners to show which piece joins up with which. Then lay the parts out, right sides together, with the edges in line. Pin them together, starting at the bottom, 1cm in from the selvedge, and with the pins every 10cm or so parallel to the selvedges. Snip the selvedges to release the tension [2.5].

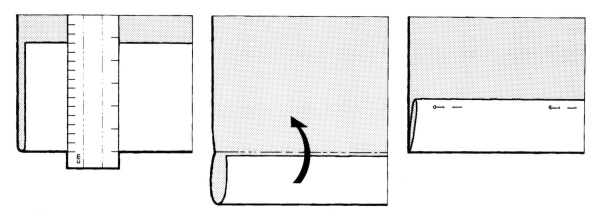

2.6a, b and c [a] Measure, [b] fold, and [c] pin the curtain hem

Sew along the line of the pins, removing them as you go. If you have pinned from the bottom, sew from the top. Alternatively, you can put the two pieces straight into the sewing-machine, using the sewing-foot as a guide to position the sewing line a constant distance from the selvedge. Make an ordinary flat seam in either case.

Joining widths of patterned fabric introduces an additional complication. In a pattern with a strongly repeated motif, you may find that you have to lose up to almost an entire pattern repeat on each curtain. If you *have* chosen a heavily patterned fabric, however, cut your first two main lengths as explained above. Then move the next part up and down against one of the lengths to work out the match. Rather than having a full width plus a part-width, you may find the answer is to have two part-widths which won't interfere with the pattern. It will be a case of trial and error in deciding where the centre seam will be so that the pattern will look the least disturbed, and you will need to bear in mind where the side hems will occur after joining the cut widths together. It is advisable to tack along the seam after pinning it, before you sew. This seam should be run-and-fell (page 12), which will have the effect of neatening the cut edges. This exercise is tricky and needs concentration.

MAKING UP THE CURTAINS

Lay one curtain out on the ironing-board, wrong side up, with the bottom edge facing you. Starting at one of the bottom corners, measure with a wooden ruler 12cm from the bottom. Turn the fabric up so that the wrong sides are together and press in a crease with the iron at a fairly cool setting. Continue along the bottom, measuring at close intervals for accuracy. That crease will form the bottom edge of the finished curtain. Any pattern should match all along the hem line.

Open out the fold. Work your way once more across the fabric with the iron, but this time fold the bottom hem in half, turning up the raw edge as accurately as possible to meet the fold you have just created. Turn the fabric up once more at the first crease, and you will have a neat double 6cm hem. Pin it in place at intervals of 10cm or so, 1cm down from the top of the hem [2.6a, b and c]. Finally, slip stitch the hem in place. If the fabric is very heavy, leave the hem till last so that it has time to hang properly.

Sew the sides next. It is preferable to do them after the hem so that the edge of the bottom hem is hidden at the sides of the curtain.

First, fold the material in by 4cm and press it. If you keep the iron fairly cool, you can use the iron to hold the material in position while you pull it out taut with one hand, and measure it with the other. Move the iron along to put in the crease.

Go back to the beginning and turn the material in to make the double thickness. This time do not fold the hem in half, but turn it in by 1.5cm, leaving a side hem of 2.5cm. Press it, pin it in place, then hand-sew it.

24

2.7   Curtain weights

Weights

Some fabrics hang better if weighted at the bottom. A good stockist will carry at least three grades of flexible weights. The correct grade to use will depend on the type of fabric and the curtain length. As a general rule, use 25g per metre weights for net curtains, 70g per metre for lightweight fabrics, and 150g per metre for heavy fabrics. Sew the sides of the curtains first; then turn up the hem and fold up and press in mitred corners. If you are using those weights that look like a string of sausages, hand-stitch along the hem, thread the weights through with the help of a safety-pin, and then close up the mitred edges. Stitch invisibly round the weights at intervals to secure them in place. Sew the coin-type of weight in the corners [2.7].

Preparing the heading

Lay one curtain wrong side up on the table or floor. Refer to your notes and recall the figure for the hook drop that you measured, and add the width of the heading tape. On the flat surface, start marking off this new measurement from the bottom of the curtain. Providing you have cut and measured everything squarely at all preceding stages, you will have a consistent length for the whole curtain. (You might think it would be easier to measure from the top down to the hook, but it is safer to do that afterwards, as a double-check.)

When you have marked off the hook drop plus the measurement of the heading, fold the fabric along this point and press it flat, just as you did the bottom hem. At this stage you may want to consider adding a certain crispness to the heading. This is done by ironing on or sewing a band of Vilene or heavyweight interfacing under the fold of the heading, the width of the curtain and 5cm deep.

Next, fix the heading tape to the curtain 2cm down from the top (1cm for pencil pleats). It is best to go across the fabric with the wooden ruler, inserting pins parallel to the top edge at the 2cm mark. Leave an overhang of 2.5cm at each side. There are two strings running through the tape. Make them secure because if they ever come loose, you will have to re-make the heading.

First, work out which is the inner edge of your curtain – the edge that will be at the centre of the window. Lift the end of the tape up to expose the underside and count back three of the small slots through which the cord runs. Pull the cord out of those three slots with the points of your scissors. Tie the two ends together securely on the underside. Fold the end of the tape under, with the knot lying underneath so that the edge of the tape lies just within the edge of the curtain [2.8a, b and c]. Pin it in place.

2.8a, b and c   Fix the heading on the inner edge of the curtain by [a] pulling the cord through to the back, [b] knotting it, and [c] folding the tape under and pinning it

25

2.9a, b and c Fix the heading on the outer edge of the curtain by [a] pulling the cord through to the front, [b] knotting it, and [c] folding the tape under and pinning it

2.10 Machine along the heading in the directions indicated

At the outer edge of the curtain, again pull out the string as far as the third hole along, but this time pull it out through the front of the tape. Knot the ends of the two cords together, but not too close to the tape. You simply need to stop the cords working their way out of the tape. Fold the tape under, just in from the edge of the curtain, and pin it in place [2.9a, b and c].

You will have to sew the tape to the heading, perfectly flat, along both its top and bottom edges, and secure it at the ends. The best way is to machine-sew along the top, turn at the corner, and sew down the end of the tape. Cut the thread. Move the material back in the machine to start again on the top, stitching 2.5cm in from the end. Sew along the top 2.5cm to the corner, turn and sew down the end, turn again and sew right across the curtain to the opposite side, turn the

material again, and sew up the opposite end to the top [2.10]. Sewing in the same direction along the two long sides prevents the fabric or the heading pulling.

All you have to do now to finish the curtain is gather it up to form the pleats. Refer to the track measurement and halve it. The curtain will have to cover this half-length. Now add 10cm to the measurement so that the two curtains will meet in the middle without straining.

Gather up the curtain on the cord to the right length. If you have no one to help you, hook the looser knot in the cord (the one you tied second) over a door-knob and pull the heading tape along the taut cord.

Some curtain-makers recommend drawing the heading tape as tight as possible on the string, then letting it out to the right length. Whichever way suits you, the pleats must be crisp and evenly formed.

With the heading gathered to the right length, tie up the loose cord into a neat coil. Do not cut it off or knot it: when you take the curtains down for washing or cleaning, you will need to flatten the heading.

You could buy a small plastic cord-tidy for coiling the loose ends of the cord, or you could wind the ends into a figure-of-eight over your fingers to make a neat bundle.

Fit the hooks at regular intervals along the heading, through the bottom set of slots. The standard recommendation is one every 7 or 8cm. If you have made a short unlined curtain in a lightweight fabric you may use fewer. A floor-length curtain in velvet, lined and interlined, would need the maximum support.

Lay the curtain out wrong side up, and hold the hook with the long point away from you facing towards the top of the curtain. Pass the long point up through the back of the slot in the heading, then turn it towards you. The curled eyes will stop it going right through the curtain, and the long point will now be downwards, ready to hook into the glider.

Insert the hooks all the way along the heading at your chosen intervals. Make sure you have hooks at the ends or as near to the ends as possible, but don't put a hook through the hole where the coiled cord emerges. Put a hook outside that cord if there is a space available.

If the track has a 'return' – in other words, bends round a short distance at each side to fit the curve of a recess – put a hook in at the very end of each curtain with the next at the corner. Don't gather up or pleat the curtain between those points. Likewise, gather up or pleat the curtain less where it will overlap with the other curtain when drawn.

If you have left the hem till last (on heavy curtains), let the curtain hang for a few days with hems unsewn. This will ensure that the bottom edge is level. You could hand-sew the hem with the curtain still hanging which will make the job less cumbersome and heavy. Mitre the bottom corners if you leave taking up the hem till last.

Now press the curtain. If it is long, place two chairs on the other side of the ironing-board ready to receive each section as you iron.

2.11   Curl outer side edge of the curtain round the track end

Hanging the curtains

Once you have made a pair of curtains, it is essential to hang them well to achieve a good 'set'. If the curtains are long, get someone to stand by the window bearing the weight of the material while you stand on a stepladder to slot the hooks through the gliders. Fit as many gliders to the track as you have hooks (consult the manufacturer's recommendation). With the hooks in place in the curtain tape, start at either end and slip the hooks into the rings. All hooks go on from the front, except those at the side edges of each curtain. Curl the side hems round and insert these outer two from the rear. It will help to give a good roll to the edge of the curtain and prevent the hems (and lining if there is one), as well as the cord-tidy or bundle of cord, showing from inside the room [2.11].

Finally, ease the gathers or pleating into place. Take a handful of the bottom hem corresponding with the material at the top, and run your cupped hand down the first fold from top to bottom. (Again you will need someone to help you on long curtains.) Push that gather or pleat across to the side and work on subsequent folds all along. To achieve an even folding, tie a piece of tape or strip of fabric round the drawn-back curtain and leave it overnight. (Do not pull too tightly on velvet as you may leave a mark.) The curtain will subsequently fall in the same folds.

MAKING LININGS

Lining fabric is a tightly woven cotton, generally beige, cream or white. Beige looks acceptable with most colours at the red end of the spectrum (yellows, browns, reds). White tends to go better with blue/green fabrics and should be used for thin materials with a white background, as coloured or beige could show through.

Linings may be permanently or temporarily attached to the curtain, or made separately on their own heading tape and attached to the same hooks as the curtain. The latter method is the most convenient, as the linings can be separated from the curtains when either lining or curtain is due for cleaning. But joining the lining to the curtain will give a better finished appearance.

Standard lining heading tape is manufactured in a 'V' shape with the two sides forming a kind of skirt. One side is slightly wider than the other, and the cord runs along the shorter side. The top edge of the lining fabric lies snugly between the two sides of the skirt [2.12]. The same hooks which carry the curtain will carry the lining. As with the curtains themselves, you will have to make left-sided and a right-sided lining.

Curtain lining usually comes in 120cm widths. This may be the same as your curtain fabric width, but if the latter is wider you will have to join widths of lining together.

To determine the amount to buy, refer to the hook drop of your curtain. Deduct 1.5cm for clearance at the bottom, because the lining will be shorter than the curtain. Add 12cm for a double 6cm hem at the bottom and 1.5cm at the top for attaching the lining fabric to the lining tape. (You could reasonably cancel out these figures and regard the total length needed as the curtain hook drop.) Then, add 10cm for possibly poor cutting in the shop. Double that figure for two curtains and finally round up to the nearest quarter metre you can buy. Amend the calculation if you need to join widths (page 23). You can minimise waste by calculating for several curtains at a time and buying one length to cut from as you need.

Spread the lining on a table or floor and cut it square at the bottom (do not use the pulled thread method). Measure and cut as many lengths as you need. Join with ordinary flat seams – press open but do not neaten.

2.12   Standard lining heading tape

2.13   Slot the hooks through the cords of both the curtain and lining headings

Turn up the bottom hem by 12cm and press it flat, then turn in the last 6cm, and press that too, to give you a double 6cm hem, as on the curtain itself. You can machine-sew this hem. Turn in, and machine-sew double hems down the sides too, the first fold being 4cm, the second 1.5cm. Mitre the corners for a neat finish.

Remembering that you need to make a left- and right-handed version, position the fabric and the lining tape on your sewing-machine, with the lining to the left and the tape to the right. Feed the lining fabric into the tape, right to the top of the divide, and sew along the top, feeding and sewing as you go. If you find that difficult, start by pinning the fabric into place in the lining tape, then remove the pins as you sew. The shorter, corded side of the tape should be on the right side of the lining [2.12].

2.14   Fixed lining

2.15   Bagged curtain

At the ends, treat the cord exactly as you treated the cord on the main part of the curtain (pages 25–6). Pull through the cord, gather up the lining to just less than the finished width of the curtain itself. Form a tidy roll in the excess part of the cord, as on the main heading.

To fit the lining, lay it out on top of the curtain so that the top cord in the lining tape coincides with the bottom cord in the heading tape. Fit the curtain hooks, but slot the hooks through both of these cords [2.13]. The lining will then hang well, with the side hems together.

Fixed lining

Because of the weight of the lining fabric on a large curtain, a detachable lining tends to droop between the hooks and hang out of true at the bottom.

You can avoid this by sewing the lining to the curtain. Make up the linings as in the previous method up to the point where you deal with the top edge. In this system it will have no separate tape. Instead, turn down the top edge to give a 3cm hem. Lay this top hem so that it just overlaps the bottom of the heading tape on the curtain, and machine-sew the two together. The sewing line should be the same as that which joins the bottom edge of the heading tape to the curtain [2.14].

The curtain and lining hang as though they were separate, but there is no chance of them gaping apart at the top. When you want to wash or clean the curtains, unpick the line of sewing, wash the linings separately and sew them together again when they are ready for re-hanging.

Bagged curtain

A third type of construction is the simple bagged curtain. It entails sewing the linings to the curtains round three sides and is useful for fairly small curtains.

Measure up and join widths as in the basic curtain process, for both the curtain and lining. Cut the curtain fabric following the formula given on page 22. Cut the lining to the length and width of what will be the finished flat curtain – i.e. the curtain's hook drop plus the heading height above the hook.

Lay the lining on the curtain, right sides together, placing the top edge of the lining 7.5cm below the top edge of the curtain. Notch the selvedges and then sew the sides together 1.5cm in from the edges, beginning at the top of the lining and finishing about 20cm from the bottom.

Turn up a double 2.5cm hem on the bottom of the lining and machine-sew it. Turn up a double 7.5cm hem on the curtain fabric and hand-sew it, mitring the corners. Turn the whole assembly inside out, and adjust the fabrics to give equal side hems to the curtain fabric. Pin and press them in place. Hand-sew the lining to the curtain as far as the bottom [2.15].

At the top, turn the curtain fabric down over the lining to give the correct curtain length. Mitre the corners and sew on the heading tape. The top edge of the lining can be left raw because it will be covered by the heading tape.

29

2.16   Locked-in lining

Locked-in lining

This is the professional way to line curtains. It is worth the extra trouble as it will greatly improve the hang of the curtains. The lining should be 8cm narrower and 4cm shorter than the finished flat curtain. Join widths and press the seams open. Press in a single 6cm hem down each side of the curtain, and a single 15cm bottom hem, with mitred corners. Secure the hems with a loose slip stitch.

Lay the curtain out on a flat surface, right side downwards. With a metre rule and dressmaker's chalk (or pins for a loose-woven fabric), draw vertical lines down the curtain at intervals of about 30cm. The intervals can be greater on a very wide curtain.

Then lay the lining on top of the curtains, wrong sides together. Fold back one edge of the lining until you can see the first chalk or pin line. Starting about 18cm from the top of the curtain, lockstitch the two pieces of fabric together, making large stitches about 10cm apart. Don't pull the threads tight, and only pick up one or two threads each time – otherwise the stitching will show on the right side of the curtain [**2.16**]. Continue until you get to the hem line of the curtain. Repeat across the curtain.

When you have locked the lining to the curtain across its entire width, turn and press the lining fabric 2cm in at the sides, and 4cm at the bottom. Slip stitch the lining to the curtain hem all round to close the hems.

Interlining

Curtains generally look perfectly acceptable if they are made with good lining. But there is a further step that gives them an extra luxurious appearance, with a roll at the edges and fullness of folding. It consists of a third layer of fabric fitted between the curtains and the lining.

Interlining is generally made of rough and soft flannel called bump or domett which provides considerable additional insulation. There is also available a metallic fabric designed specifically as a heat insulator. You can use this as a lining – but interlining may still be necessary to improve the look of the curtains.

Cut the interlining to the same dimensions as the main fabric. You may need to join widths, in which case use a run-and-fell seam, as interlining tends to stretch.

Deal with the interlining before the lining. Spread out the unsewn curtain right side down with the interlining on top of it, matching the bottom and side edges. Fold the interlining in half and lockstitch it to the curtain down the fold line. Make other rows of lockstitching *across* the curtain at intervals of about 30cm, depending on the width of the fabric.

Then fold in about 5cm at the bottom and each side, treating the curtain fabric and interlining as one. Mitre the corners – you could trim away the interlining here to reduce bulk. Slip stitch the hems and corners in place.

Now lay the lining on top of the interlined curtain and continue as if you were lining a curtain in the ordinary way.

2.17   A range of pelmet designs

PELMETS AND VALANCES

There was a time when pelmets were considered too fussy and everybody seemed to prefer the uncluttered lines of a simple decorative heading.

However, the pelmet is especially suitable for large windows in Georgian or Victorian houses, and it is an excellent device for linking two windows. It can also disguise poorly proportioned windows if it is mounted higher or lower than the window frame or extended at the sides.

Basically, the pelmet is a shaped piece of buckram covered with fabric and mounted on to a shelf, concealing the curtain track. It can be straight-edged or shaped. Usually it is covered with the same fabric as the one used to make the curtains or blind, but it is possible to achieve dramatic effects with a contrasting fabric. You can produce a softer line by fitting interlining material between the buckram and the fabric. A good pelmet starts with the design. The choice runs from a straight, unfussy version, through a variety of more or less simple curves, to the elaborate kind of design shown last [2.17].

For a softer line you could consider making a frilled valance – they performance much the same function in concealing the curtain track while giving a good design finish to the window. They may be lined but are often left unlined to take advantage of their frilly and billowing appearance. They are especially suitable on cottage and bedroom windows, particularly in an informal patterned print or chintz.

A valance is far simpler to make than a pelmet. It can be nailed to a board, just as a pelmet is, or fitted to a track separate from the curtains with its own hooks and rings.

Making the pelmet board

This is really just like putting up a shelf. You need a piece of wood, hardboard or plywood, 10–15cm wide, 15–20mm thick, and long enough to cover the window and just clear the curtains at the end (5cm would be enough unless you want to alter the window's proportions).

Pelmets are sometimes given vertical wooden 'returns' which make the structure into a sort of box, but a simple shelf is perfectly adequate. If you are fitting a pelmet into a recess you won't need returns. If you are fitting a pelmet round a bay, you will either have to shape and plane the wood to follow the curve, or buy the pelmet board ready-made.

Fix brackets to the wall with enough screws to bear the weight of the board itself, plus the curtains, plus any stress that will occur when the curtains are drawn.

The track should be fixed to the underside of the pelmet board. Almost all types of track have fittings which can be screwed on horizontally or vertically. The vertical arrangement suits the pelmet.

One advantage of the pelmet system over plain tracks is that you can arrange the tracks with one overlapping the other by about 15cm: this gives a better line than the alternative of bending one of the tracks. It is also possible to buy fittings which hold the edge of the curtain out to produce an overlap. They are a perfectly good choice and you need then only fit one continuous length of track. Try the board in place for measurement. Then take it down to fit the pelmet fabric to it.

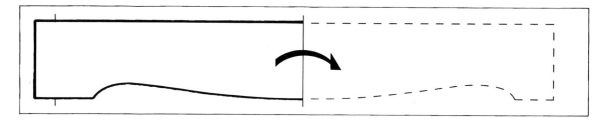

2.18 Turn the template over to get a mirror image. Mark the centre point and the start of the returns

2.19 Joining sections of pelmet fabric

2.20 Assembling the buckram and covering fabric

Making up the pelmet

To make the pelmet itself, you will need a length of good quality buckram. To establish its length, measure along the pelmet board and add the lengths of the two returns (the pelmet will have returns even if the board doesn't). Its depth will be the greatest depth on your design – normally this will be the same depth as the returns. It is not good design to have any point on the front of the pelmet hanging lower than the returns, and the returns themselves should be straight, front-to-back. Make a template from brown paper of half your finished design, from one side to the centre. Try it at the window before laying it on the buck-

ram. Remember to add the length of the return at the end. With dressmaker's chalk and on both sides of the buckram, draw round the design, turn the template over on its end, and repeat the process for the other side. Mark clearly the centre and the points where the returns start [**2.18**]. To join lengths of buckram, butt them together and apply another short length of buckram at the back. Dampen the contact surfaces with a sponge and go over the area with a hot iron, covering the buckram with brown paper first to prevent the glue side transferring to the iron. Cut out the buckram.

If the pelmet needs more than one width of fabric, first fit a complete width in the centre. Then, patterns matching if necessary, cut another width in half and fit one half either side of the centre panel [2.19]. Sew the seams right sides together and press open.

Lay the buckram on the fabric and cut round it, leaving a 2.5cm margin or fabric for working, and 2.5cm at each end in addition to the length of the returns. The buckram will probably curve, however long you leave it unrolled. Use the concave side of the curve as the front of the pelmet: that will eventually give a better 'set' to the finished job, particularly at the corners.

If you plan to use interlining, fit it at this stage. Lay bump or domett over the front of the buckram, butting any joints to make up the full width and trim it to the exact shape of the buckram. Use a warm iron with brown paper and the melted glue from the buckram will fix the bump in place. Check that it is accurately trimmed.

With your covering fabric seamed, cut out and the selvedge removed, locate the centre and mark it with pins at the top and bottom. If the fabric is plain, fold it in two to find the centre.

Lay the fabric on the buckram and pin the two firmly together at the exact centre, top and bottom. The task now is to smooth the fabric over the buckram, without pulling it off centre, or distorting the fabric, and without wrinkling it.

Sewing it gives a softer line: using doubled cotton and starting centre top, turn the allowance over evenly to the back of the buckram and tack right along the top of the pelmet. Stretch the fabric outwards as you go, to give a taut finish. When you get to the end, secure and break the thread, go back to the centre and sew outwards to the other side [2.20].

For the bottom edge, snip the fabric to go round all the convex curves, and cut small wedges into the corners [2.20]. The skill is in pulling and cutting the fabric enough to take out all the tension and puckering, while not cutting so far that the buckram shows and the fabric frays. Tack it with the same stitch as the straight top edge. Trim the vertical ends of the fabric to about 1.5cm and turn them in.

Fixing the pelmet

What you do next depends on whether you plan

2.21a and b Permanent methods of fixing a pelmet: [a] Hammer in tacks, or [b] use heading tape and drawing pins

to fix the pelmet permanently or make it detachable for dry-cleaning. If it is to be a permanent fixture there are two alternatives. You can line it first, fix it to the board along the top and sides with metal tacks, and then glue on the braid to cover the tacks [2.21a]. Alternatively, you can sew on the braid or fringe, and line the pelmet so that the stitching is concealed. Then apply a length of curtain heading tape of a matching colour (turning under the raw ends) by sewing down the tape at intervals of about 10cm, making sure that the stitching does not go through to the front fabric [2.21b]. You can then push a drawing-pin through the heading tape into the edge of the

2.22a and b Temporary methods of fixing a pelmet: [a] Hook rings over nails, or [b] use Velcro strips

At whichever stage you apply the lining, you need to cut lining fabric to the same shape as the pelmet but add on seam allowances of 1cm all round. Pin it centrally in position, then slip stitch round, snipping into the allowance to ease any curves. Neither stitching nor lining fabric should be visible from the front. Then, attach the pelmet by your chosen method.

Valances

A simple valance is a length of fabric gathered into a series of frills, or more formally drawn up into a series of triple or pinch pleats. The depth of valance is generally between one-sixth and one-ninth the distance from curtain rail to floor. Add 12cm for a 3–5cm heading and the hem at the bottom. Cut and sew fabric to make up the width: not less than 1½ times the distance across the front of the curtains, plus the returns. Thin flimsy fabrics may need more than this, while heavier ones will hang awkwardly if too much is used.

Making up the valance for fitting to a rail is nearly the same as making up a curtain. Turn down the top hem and sew on a simple heading tape. Check the height of the valance, and turn up a small double hem at the bottom to the depth you want. Draw up the valance to the appropriate length and insert hooks to fit the curtain rail, including fixed ones at each end [2.23a].

An alternative type has a pencil pleated heading. Use one of the special types of tape with its correct hooks. The valance can be fixed on to a valance rail or a pelmet board. If you are fitting it to a board, screw small eye hooks along the front edge of the board at intervals to correspond with the hooks in the tape [2.23b].

The other way to deal with the valance is to enclose the top raw edge in bias binding, and then hammer tacks through the binding all along the board [2.23c].

If the fabric is not sufficiently firm, make up a length of interfacing, deep enough to fit from the top of the finished valance to the bottom of the heading tape – this will provide the necessary 'body'. Lockstitch it into place as described on page 30, and finally sew it when you sew on the heading tape.

board at the centre of each 'pocket'.

The alternatives if you want the pelmet to be removable are to trim and line it, then sew on small brass or plastic rings at each end, and hammer nails into the edges of the returns to correspond [2.22a]. The fit must be taut or the pelmet will sag where it has no attachment along the front.

Otherwise glue a strip of Velcro to each side of the board and sew on the corresponding strip to the return of the pelmet [2.22b]. Do this after applying the trimming and lining.

2.23a, b and c Methods of attaching a valance: [a] Hooked to the curtain rail. [b] Hooked to screw eyes. [c] Bias binding with tacks hammered through

Some fabrics are so soft that it is worth lining the valance as well as stiffening the heading with interfacing. If you are using all the choices – fabric, interfacing, interlining and lining – cut the interfacing and interlining to the finished length and depth of the valance. First fit the interfacing in place, then the interlining. Lockstitch the interlining to the interfacing at intervals of about 30cm. Lockstitch the lining to the interlining at similar intervals.

Turn in the allowances of the lining and fabric, and slip stitch along the top, bottom and ends. Then sew on the heading tape following the directions on page 25.

SWAGS AND TAILS

These are an elaborate extension of the pelmet or valance, and are appropriate on tall windows only. They are sometimes called draperies or draped pelmets. The style was popular in Victorian and Edwardian residences, and the most suitable fabrics are correspondingly luxurious – satin, velvet and taffeta, for instance. Modern synthetic fabrics would also be possible. Avoid stiff fabrics as they don't hang well. The swags and tails will probably be of the same fabric as the curtains.

They use a lot of material, so calculate carefully before embarking on a scheme which calls for their extensive use. Have a rehearsal beforehand with lengths of muslin or an old, well-ironed sheet.

Swags
The swag – the part that hangs in folds across the top of the curtains – is fixed to the same kind of board as a pelmet, so carry out the woodwork and attach the curtain track to it before you start.

Then consider the proportions of the swag. The taller the window the deeper the swag. On a narrow window, a single swag may be all that is needed. A wide window may be able to carry a set of three or perhaps even five, overlapping so that alternate ones emerge from behind the others. Make sure they overlap at a good clear angle – the effect of the swags will be lost if they appear to merge into one continuous run.

Two important factors are the angle of the sides of the pattern from the vertical, and the shape of the curved bottom edge. If the angle is acute, and the curve pronounced, the folds of the finished swag will be deep. If shallow, the finished folds on the swag will also be shallow. You will find out what is best for your window when experimenting with the muslin.

2.24a and b A typical swag: [a] Opened flat. [b] With pinned pleats

You will need to measure and mark the points down the sides of the swag at which the folds will occur. Folding points at intervals of 15–18cm are right for most purposes. The best effect is achieved by a small number of pronounced folds rather than several skimpy ones.

When you have outlined the pattern, cut out the fabric. Cut half of the pattern, then double the fabric along its length and cut the other half to achieve a neat symmetrical curve; or fold the fabric parallel to the selvedges before you cut. The approximate shape of the swag's pattern will be as in [**2.24a**]. Cut an identical piece of lining fabric and sew it to the main fabric, right sides together, down the two sides and along the bottom. Trim the corners, neaten the seams, and then turn the fabrics right sides out.

Transfer the planned pleating points from the pattern along the two sides. Starting from the top, pin each pleat in place [**2.24b**]. Try the swag in position. Then sew the pleats firmly into place, and attach the swag to the board along the top edge by hammering in tacks, having turned under the top raw edge.

2.25a and b A tail: [a] The pattern. [b] Folded

2.26   A pleated centre tail

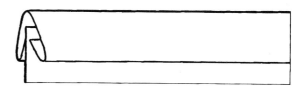

2.27   The tops of swags and tails enclosed in a double folded band

Tails

Tails invariably accompany swags to break the line at the edge of the window; they are sometimes incorporated along the window to trim the junctions between swags.

They may be in the same fabric as the swags and the curtains but you could use contrasting fabrics. Tails should be lined on the reverse side because parts will show from the front. The lining could be the same or a contrasting fabric.

The pattern for a tail is shown in [**2.25a**]. There will be one at each side of the curtain so cut reverse pairs. This type of tail is not normally used between swags. You may choose between a straight line along the bottom edge, or a convex or concave curve. A concave curve will reveal more of the reverse side of the fabric. The angle of the bottom will alter the sets of the swags. Experiment with bits of muslin for effects produced by various patterns.

Make five marks at equal intervals along the top of the edge of the pattern to divide it into six sections. Fold the sections mark-to-mark, as shown in [**2.25b**]. When you have determined your pattern, cut the matching pair from your finished fabric. Sew fabric to lining, right sides together, round the sides and bottom edge. Trim the corners of the seam to avoid bulk and turn the tail right side out. Fold it into the pleats. Sew the top edge to the finished shape, and fit it to the swag board by turning under the top raw edge and hammering in a couple of tacks.

Pleated centre tails

The traditional means of trimming the curtain between the swags includes several versions of a short centre tail, cut symmetrically.

A plain pleated centre tail is shown in [**2.26**]. Ideally, the lowest point should be no longer than the shortest pleat on the outside tails. Cut and line the fabric, turn it inside out and fold it into pleats as indicated by the marks.

All swags and tails can be finished by sewing them into a contrasting band of fabric, double-folded to form two double hems so that all the raw edges are enclosed within it [**2.27**]. The band can then be turned over the top of the swag fixing board, and tacked or pinned in place. You could also attach tassels or cord as further embellishments.

NET CURTAINS

Net curtains are most commonly used for maintaining privacy and hiding an ugly view, while letting in the light. In some circumstances you might use café curtains or a blind instead.

A variety of manufactured heading tapes are now made specifically for use with nets. You will need a rail with hooks and rings for fitting the net, so that method is probably more suited to larger windows where the heading will be high enough to be obscured. Fit whichever heading tape you choose as if you were making ordinary curtains.

For smaller windows, the old-fashioned method of sewing a casing into the net for slotting through a plastic-coated wire is simple and unobtrusive. Nets normally hang within the window recess. Cut the wire to give just enough tension so that it holds taut. Insert two cuphooks into the window frame at the sides and two eyes into the ends of the wire rod. Fit the wire 2.5cm down from the top of the available space for the net to allow room for the heading.

Measure the length of the curtain from the wire to the window sill, or to the bottom of the frame, according to your preference and the type of window. The width of the curtain should be up to 1½ times the width of the window.

Allow a total of 6cm for two doubled 1.5cm side hems. To the finished length of fabric, add 7.5cm at the top for the casing and heading, and 15cm at the bottom for a double 7.5cm hem.

Because the net is translucent, any joins will show slightly. Join widths with either a French or a run-and-fell seam (pages 10–12). The seam must of course be on the wrong side of the fabric. Use a fine no 9 sewing-machine needle and a fairly large stitch. It helps to insert layers of tissue paper between the layers of net to prevent them slipping around while you are sewing.

Sew the two side hems first, each a doubled 1.5cm. Then turn up and sew the bottom double 7.5cm hem. Add any weights at this stage – the string-of-sausages type are the best ones for net curtains. At the top, turn down the fabric at the 7.5cm mark, and fold under the first 2.5cm. Sew the fold down to the fabric, then sew along the line just below the raw edge, to produce a heading of 2.5cm, and a casing of about 2.5cm. Thread the net on to the wire.

2.28 Pattern for a draped net curtain

2.29 Attaching a frilled hem to a net curtain

Draped nets

The type of net draped to the sides of the window is especially effective on large and full-length windows.

If necessary, join widths to give adequate fullness, using a narrow French or run-and-fell seam. To determine the number of widths to use, divide the window width into three. Each curtain occupies two thirds of that width, so that they overlap across the middle third of the window. Use 2–2½ times the finished width in each curtain.

The fabric must be cut to accommodate the additional length, so the pattern for cutting will be longer on one side than on the other [**2.28**]. To calculate these lengths, pin a piece of string to the window frame at point A, drape it loosely to the point where the tie-back will hold it, and let it hang to the sill or floor, depending on where the bottom hem of the curtain will fall, B. The other side is a straight measurement.

Add 7.5cm for the heading and casing, and 2.5cm for a double hem at the bottom. Make a pair of curtains to mirror each other for opposite sides. Because of the overlap, you will need two plastic-coated wires to hang the curtains on, but you can fix them to the same hooks at the sides of the window frame.

The curtains need tie-backs to hold them in the draped position. Cut a piece of plain net 10cm wide and 30cm long. Turn in the ends by 1.5cm and fold the sides to the centre. This will give a strip 2.5cm wide and 27cm long. Close the ends and open side by slip stitching, and sew a small ring to each end for fitting over a hook.

Nets with a frilled hem

Many nets come with the frill already attached, but to make one, cut four long strips of net each 12cm wide and the length of the inner side hem.

Join two of the strips together and fold the resulting strip lengthwise to enclose the short seam. Then fold in the two long edges and make two rows of gathers along that edge.

Give the curtains a double 1.5cm hem along the bottom and up the outside edges. Press down the top hem to form the 2.5cm casing and the 2.5cm heading, or attach heading tapes.

The inside edge is the important one. Draw the frill up on its gathering threads to this length. Lay the frill parallel to the curtain, about a centimetre in from the edge and starting it 2.5cm from the top so that it doesn't get in the way of the casing [**2.29**]. Sew the two together, right sides together, then turn the longer seam allowance of the curtain over the frill's raw edges. Press down the seam.

2.30 Sew across the piping to hem a festoon net

2.31 Anchor the festoons by sewing through each pinning point

Festoon nets

Billowing festoon nets provide privacy but admit light, and give a softness of line which is perhaps particularly suited to bedrooms. In living-rooms, a large floor-length window may be necessary to do justice to the effect. It is best to look on them as a permanent feature – if you want something similar that can be lowered and raised, Austrian or festoon blinds might be more suitable.

Festoon nets take a lot of fabric. You will need at least 1½ times the width and up to three times the height of the window.

First, calculate the dimensions. Take, for example, a 120cm wide window. It gives four 30cm festoons. To make up, festoons require casings, formed on the wrong side of the net, on which to draw up the fabric. The points at which to make these casings should be 30, 60 and 90cm across the curtain after the fabric is drawn up to the finished width. Take account of the side hems in your calculations. If you need to join widths, make run-and-fell seams that coincide with the casings.

Start by sewing the vertical casings into the length of the netting. Make two lines of stitching about 1.5cm apart. Cut lengths of piping cord the length of the window. Thread the piping into the casings with a safety pin.

Turn down and sew the top of the net to make the double heading which will be the casing for the wire, sewing across the piping cord as you go. Pin up the bottom hem and sew it in place, again going across the piping to fix it [**2.30**]. Adjust the fabric bunched up by the piping – you may find this easier if you lay the curtain out on the floor. At intervals of 10 or 12cm down each vertical casing, pin the folds to the piping – the pinning points must all be level. Insert the wire through the top casing, and try the curtain up against the window to see if the festoons are hanging neatly and equally. When you are satisfied, take the curtain down and sew through each pinning point to anchor the festoons in place [**2.31**].

Sew any fringes or tassels to the hem or the bottoms of the vertical casings, and the curtain is now ready to hang properly.

It is also possible to buy a narrow lightweight nylon gathering tape, which you can simply sew on to the back of the curtain at the required intervals, then pull up the net to give the festoons.

TIE-BACKS

The appearance of some curtains and bed hangings is improved by the use of tie-backs. Tasselled silk rope is available in many colours, but a more individual approach would be to make your own, either in the same fabric as the curtain or a contrasting one. The tie-back is generally stiffened with interlining and it could be lined on the reverse.

Hold a fabric tape measure round the open, or partially open, curtain as if the tape measure were the tie-back. If the curtains are floor-length, the tie-back would be level with the bottom of the window. Don't pull the curtain too tightly as it will hang wrongly and may even mark the fabric.

Note the length required and add on 2cm or so for turnings. At the same time, mark in pencil the point on the wall where you want the hook to go, and fix it in place.

Cut out two strips of fabric for each tie-back, or one strip each of main fabric and lining material. They should be about 12cm deep (including seam allowances) and the length already established.

If you want rounded or pointed ends, shape the material accordingly.

Cut a piece of interfacing to the finished dimension of the tie-back. Tack it to the back of the main fabric and catch-stitch it in position.

Pin and tack the other strip to the first strip, right sides together, and then machine-sew all the way round leaving an opening of about 10cm down one long side. Grade the seams and clip the corners and any curves.

Turn the tie-back right sides out through the opening, press it and slip stitch the gap closed.

Sew on a ring at each end to fit on to the hook fixed to the wall.

CAFÉ CURTAINS

Café curtains are an attractive and well-established way of dressing a window. They fit over the bottom half of the window which gives privacy to people sitting in the room, traditionally, of course, to diners eating at café tables. At the same time they let in daylight through the top half of the window. In some circumstances you could consider them as an alternative to net curtains.

Café curtains look especially good on sash windows where the frame is divided by a horizontal bar. The curtains can be fitted to the height of this bar for a neat visual effect. You could consider hanging café curtains with a matching pelmet.

There are many ways of making café curtains. Most types fit into two end sockets, after the curtain is hung on it, or you can use other arrangements. A d-i-y or department store should be able to provide you with a good range of rods and fittings.

One of the simplest methods is to attach clip-on rings through which the pole is slotted. You make up the curtain in the usual way, but also turn down the top heading into a double hem, forming mitred corners there too. Then clip on the rings at regular intervals across the top. Or you can sew large curtain rings along the top edge, at intervals of about 10cm, with a neat buttonhole stitch [2.32a, b and c]. Again, the top hem should be completed first in the same way as the bottom hem.

A cased heading is the next easiest method and suitable for sheer fabrics.

2.32a, b and c   Hanging café curtains: [a] Use sewn rings. [b] Use clip-on rings. [c] Sew rings on to a scalloped edge

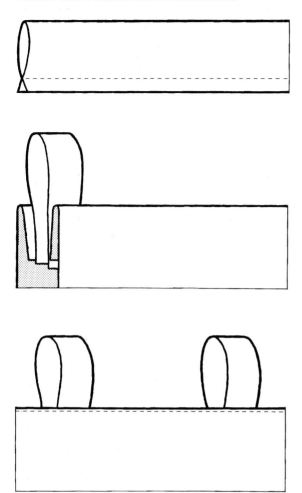

2.33a, b and c   Café curtains with tabs along the top
edge: [a] Make the tab. [b] Insert the tab between curtain
fabric and lining. [c] Tabs stitched into position

A method more usually associated with café
curtains is to sew tabs along the top edge for the
pole to go through.

Make up the basic curtain first. The length will
be from a point about 7.5cm below the rod to the
bottom point of the finished curtain. Add 15cm
for a double 7.5cm bottom hem, and 2.5cm for a
top hem. Café curtains should not be too full, so
1½ times the width of the pole is ample. Add
10cm for a double 2.5cm hem at each side.

Café curtains look best from the outside if they
are lined – the bagged type of lining (see page 29)
works well. Make up the curtains except for the
top edge.

Make the tabs from the same fabric as the curtains. Cut enough tabs to fit at 15cm intervals
along the width of the curtain. Measure the circumference of the pole, add on a total of 2.5cm
for seam allowances and another 5cm for movement. This will be the length of the piece of material to cut for each tab. The finished width will
be about 6 or 7cm, so double that for the two sides
and add 2.5cm for seam allowances.

Fold each piece in two along its length, right
sides together, without creasing the fold. Sew
along the seam 1.5cm in from the edge [2.33a].
Open out the seam and press it. Turn the tab
inside out, position the seam down the centre of
the tab, and press down the side folds. Press the
seam allowances of the curtain and its lining in
towards each other by 2.5cm. Pin the tabs 15cm
apart and ensure that all the raw edges are
enclosed – allow a 1.25cm seam allowance at each
end of the tab [2.33b].

Try the curtain on the pole to see that all the
tabs lie comfortably. Then remove it and stitch
along the top edge of the curtain so that the tabs
are fixed in place and the top edge is closed
[2.33c].

Scalloped café curtains
Another popular style is one in which the fabric
itself is cut in a scalloped pattern and the curtain
is hung on the rod with a set of rings.

The curtains are best lined (although see below
for how to make facings for the scalloped edge if
you don't want to line them). In this case they
should be barely wider than the window – otherwise the effect of the scallops will be lost. 1¼
times the width of the curtain would be appropriate. Add 2.5cm for the side seams. The total
height (which will include the scallops) will be
from about 3cm below the pole to the sill, plus
2.5cm for turnings.

Join the fabric and lining, right sides together,
down the sides. Trim the seams, but don't turn
the tube inside out. Pin the top edges together.

Then make a template for the scallops. The
general width is about 8cm with about 3cm in between each scallop, but the dimensions of the
curtain will dictate their exact width and
positioning. If you have difficulty dividing the
curtain into these measurements, the two end
spaces can be increased. Draw a circle with a pair

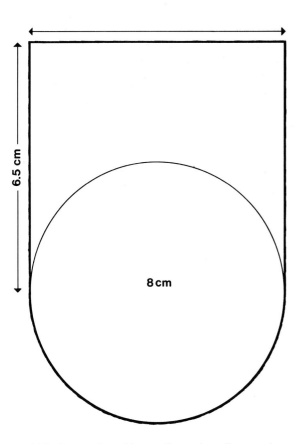

2.34   Pattern for making a café curtain scallop template

2.35a, b and c   Making lined, scalloped café curtains: [a] Mark the positions of the scallops. [b] Stitch round and clip curves. [c] Alternatively, make a facing and hem it

of compasses – the radius should be 4cm. Draw horizontally across the diameter and from each end draw vertical lines 6.5cm long [**2.34**].

On the lining side, mark in pencil the position of each scallop. Mark a line parallel to the top edge, 1.25cm in [**2.35a**]. Then sew round the markings [**2.35b**]. Clip into the curves and cut off the corners so that the scallops will lie flat. Turn the curtain inside out and press it carefully, especially round the scallops. Sew a curtain ring to the centre of each space between the scallops. Turn up the bottom hems to the correct height, slip stitch them together and press them.

If you don't want a lining, cut some material for facing the scallops. It should extend a couple of centimetres below them.

Join the facing to the main fabric down the side seams as before. Then draw in the scallop positions and sew them before hemming the bottom of the facing, and the sides and bottom of the fabric, with double 2.5cm hems [**2.35c**].

SHOWER CURTAINS

Shower curtains differ from other curtains in several ways – they aren't as full; they have a minimum of stitching because PVC and other waterproof fabrics tear rather easily; they need only single hems because the fabric doesn't fray, and the hooks or loops for fixing them to the shower rail are specific for the purpose.

You will need fabric up to $1\frac{1}{2}$ times the width of the area to screen, plus 2.5cm for each side hem or joined width (allow extra for matching patterns). The length will be from just beneath the shower rail to the floor, plus 2.5cm for the hem and 4 or 5cm for the top turning. (You could dispense with side and bottom hems.) You will also need a very fine sewing-machine needle and a special eyelet punch (obtainable from large haberdashery departments). Adhesive tape or paper clips will be a help too. Buy sufficient hooks for every 15cm along the top of the curtain.

Join any widths in run-and-fell seams, using a longish stitch. If making hems, turn in and sew down the sides and along the bottom of the curtain, producing single 2.5cm hems, and mitre the two bottom corners. Turn over the top hem by 4 or 5cm and secure it temporarily with tape or paper clips. During the sewing process, sprinkling a little talcum powder on the fabric will help prevent it sticking.

With the eyelet punch make holes 15cm apart along that hem. Peel off the tape or remove the clips. Insert the special hooks and hang the curtain from the shower rail [2.36].

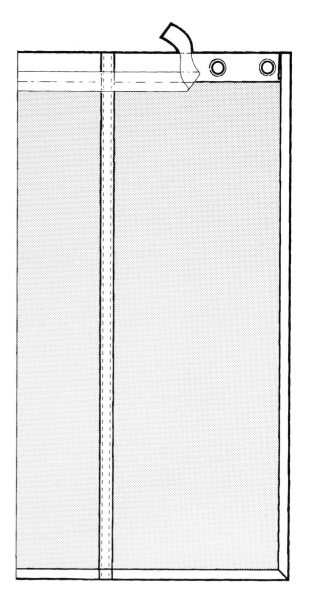

2.36 Shower curtain sewn with run-and-fell seam. Use adhesive tape instead of tacking. Use an eyelet punch for the hook holes

BLINDS

As an alternative to curtains, blinds offer several advantages. They need less fabric than curtains. When pulled up they let in more light than a drawn-back curtain, so are particularly useful in situations where you need maximum daylight. Furthermore, because they draw up out of the way, they do not obstruct desks or worktops where curtains might be inconvenient.

Roller and Roman blinds which leave the fabric flat can show patterned fabrics in quite a different way from curtains.

Roller blinds

They are uncluttered to look at and easy to clean, especially if made from plastic-coated fabrics, and are particularly suitable for bathrooms and kitchens. They can be used on their own or in conjunction with curtains, and are ideal for dormer windows or those set into sloping eaves.

You will need a roller blind kit and sufficient suitable fabric. The kit contains a wooden roller which the fabric winds round; the roller has a square pin at one end which controls the winding mechanism and a round pin at the other. The round pin comes separately so that you can cut the roller to the size required and then hammer the pin into place. Both pins fit into brackets fixed to either side of the top of the window. Also in the kit is a wooden batten which is sewn or glued at the bottom of the blind; a cord holder and length of cord for fixing to the middle of the batten; and a cord pull.

The best fabric for the purpose is holland cloth which is stiff enough, does not fray or fade, and can be sponged. It also comes in wide widths which will eliminate the need for joins. PVC is particularly suitable for kitchens and bathrooms where condensation may be a problem.

Other fabrics can be used but ought to be stiffened, either by dipping them into a special liquid sold alongside the roller blind kits, or by painting or spraying them on both sides. Try to choose a fabric that is wide enough. If the material is plain it might be possible to use it sideways. Joins can be made (by overlapping the edges by about 1cm once you have stiffened the fabric, being careful to match any pattern, and then glueing the edges together) but are rather obvious when light comes through the blind. You should also test the fabric to see how it responds to dipping, painting or spraying before buying enough to make the blind. In any case you should stiffen the fabric *before* cutting it out since many materials shrink slightly in the process.

It is also possible to buy iron-on or self-adhesive stiffening backings. These are only suitable for small blinds as the added bulk might jam the winding mechanism on a larger blind. Iron or press the backing on to the wrong side of the fabric, starting at the centre so that you can smooth any wrinkles outwards.

Use a metal or wooden rule to measure the window to find out how much material and which size kit to buy. Measure the width of window, deciding whether you want the blind to fit within it or extend a little on either side. If it is to go beyond the recess, allow at least 2.5cm at each side so that direct light is excluded.

To the length of the window add 30cm to allow for the batten casing and for the roller to remain covered when the shade is pulled right down. If the blind is to be fitted outside the recess, add on another 5cm at the top so that direct light cannot come in above the window.

Buy material to the total length of the blind (doubled if you are having to join widths) but allow a good 20cm extra to both dimensions if you are using anything other than holland or PVC, to allow for shrinkage in the course of stiffening. You do not need to take into account any side hems because stiffened fabric does not fray.

Stiffen the fabric, if necessary, before cutting or joining. When cutting, use the batten as a guideline for marking the fabric and take care to cut all the corners to an exact 90-degree angle, using a set square. Examine the fabric to see that any motifs are centrally placed and that any obvious pattern repeat will fall evenly from side to side, and also neatly at the bottom of the blind when it is unfurled. If the fabric has to be joined, it is better to have a seam at either side to balance the general appearance, particularly if the motifs are sizeable.

Attach the fixtures above the window, checking that the exact distance between them will marry with the width of the fabric. It is normal to fix the square-footed bracket to the left of the window and the round-footed one to the right,

2.37   The lower edge casing for a roller blind batten

2.38   Fix the blind squarely to the roller with tacks

which allows the blind to roll up behind the roller at the top. This means that the wrong side of the fabric will be visible round the roller when the blind is up. If you feel that this would be unaesthetic, reverse the fittings.

Next decide on the position of the batten. Either at the very bottom which is straightforward; or a short way from the bottom which will allow for a variety of decorative hems. Saw the batten to the correct length.

For the first alternative you can either glue the batten to the wrong side, glue its other side and then roll the bottom up so that the batten is enclosed (weight it while the glue dries); or you can make a casing by turning up a hem on the wrong side and stitching across to fit snugly round the batten [2.37]. You don't need to form a double hem as the material won't fray, but you do need to make the stitching absolutely straight.

If you decide upon a decorative hem, make the casing about 10cm up from the bottom of the blind – this measurement will depend on the overall proportions. If you don't want to interrupt an obvious pattern, sew a gusset of extra material to the back of the blind – again the stitching must be absolutely straight.

To fix the top end of the fabric to the roller, draw a line across the roller (if there isn't one

marked already). Line up the fabric with this guideline and secure it with adhesive tape as a trial run. The fabric should be stuck wrong side up if the square pin occurs on the left, right side up if the square pin occurs on the right.

When you are happy that the blind lies squarely tack the fabric to the roller with small tacks (these may come with the kit) [2.38].

Form any decorative bottom edging before screwing the cord holder to the centre of the batten, following the kit's instructions.

Roman blinds

Roman blinds are easy to make and do not require specially stiffened fabric. They are lined, and pull up into pleats at the top of the window by a cord mechanism sewn to the back of the blind.

You will need enough fabric and lining material to cover the window frame, plus 2.5cm at each side and a total of 15cm added to the length for the heading and hem. Adjust the total if a large pattern will need centring or lining up with the bottom. You will also have to calculate how many rings (brass or plastic) you will need, given that there will be one every 15cm vertically up the blind and one every 30cm across the blind. Also buy enough binding tape for the number of rows of rings across the blind multiplied by the height of the blind, measured from the batten.

Other requirements are enough non-stretch cord double the height of each row *plus* the distance from the top of each row to the side [2.39]; a screw eye large enough to take the cords (the one at the side where they all converge will probably have to be larger); a cleat for winding the cords round when the blind is raised; a metal rod or wooden batten the width of the blind; a piece of wood measuring 2.5cm × 5cm × the width of the blind; and two brackets and screws for fixing the heading board to the top of the window frame.

Cut out the fabric and the lining, first making sure that they are completely straight. The dimensions will be the height and width of the finished blind, plus 5cm for the side turnings and 15cm for the top and bottom. Pin them together, right sides facing, and tack round all sides except the top; check that there is no slack before machine-sewing 12mm in from the edges. Trim the corners, turn the bag inside out and press it.

Lay the blind out flat with the lining upper-

2.40 The roman blind is fixed to the headboard by a row of tacks

2.39 Roman blind: How the rings and cords are arranged over the back of the blind

2.41 Anchor the bottom of each cord by knotting it under the bottom ring

most. Using the batten as a ruler, mark in faint pencil two lines parallel to the bottom, the first 14cm from the bottom, and the next just far enough away so that when the casing is sewn the batten or rod will fit comfortably, but not loosely, within it.

Then draw vertical lines across the blind, at intervals of about 30cm, starting at the casing and continuing up to the top. The width of the blind will dictate the actual distance between the rows, but there should be a row 1cm from each edge.

Tack the tape along these lines, turning in the raw edges at top and bottom. Machine-stitch through all thicknesses down each side of the tape. Slip stitch the ends together, then sew the horizontal batten lines.

Hand-stitch on the rings at intervals of 15cm up each row, making sure that they are quite level across the blind [2.39].

Then unpick one side seam of the casing, slot

in the batten or rod and slip stitch the ends back together.

Fix the screw eyes to the underside of the head board so that they will line up with the rows of rings on the blind. The larger eye should be at the right-hand side as you face the window. Then hammer in tacks through the top of the blind to the top of the board [2.40].

Cut the cords to the correct length. This will be double the height of the blind plus the distance along the top from that particular row to the larger screw eye. Then thread the cords through the rings [2.41]. Knot them all together just beyond the larger screw eye and again at their ends, trimming them to the same length.

Fix the brackets and the heading board above the window, and screw the cleat to the wall at a comfortable height. Draw up the blind into its folds. It is best if you can keep the blind raised for a couple of days to set the pleats.

47

Austrian or festoon blinds

These blinds work on the same principle as Roman blinds but are not usually lined. They pull up into soft scalloped frills, and the heading is either gathered or pleated, as on a curtain, and the hem sometimes given an extra frill.

Measure the width of the window and double it, adding on 3 or 4cm to the total for side hems. Then measure the height of the window and add 20cm to allow for the heading and hem. Add on another 10cm if you want to have a frill.

From these measurements you will be able to estimate the amount of fabric to buy. If you need to join widths, use French seams (see page 10) as they are the neatest.

You will also need plastic or brass rings, 2cm-wide binding tape, non-stretch cord, screw eyes, a piece of wood for the heading board, two brackets to mount the board, and a cleat, exactly as for Roman blinds. A further requirement is heading tape for gathered or pencil pleats to the width of the window plus turnings, and an appropriate number of hooks and gliders.

Cut out the fabric to the dimensions required and turn in double 1.5cm side hems. Sew the frill to the bottom edge if you are having one, or hem the bottom in conjunction with the sides so that you can mitre the corners.

To make a frill, cut a length of fabric 10cm deep and twice the finished width of the blind. If necessary, join strips in an ordinary flat seam; press the turnings open. Press the frill in half lengthwise, wrong sides together, and gather along the raw edges. Draw the frill up in even gathers to fit the blind and pin it along the bottom edge, right sides together, so that the blind extends a centimetre beyond the frill. Machine-sew 1cm in from the edge of the frill. Trim the frill's edge, then turn the other edge down over the seam to neaten it.

Continue as for Roman blinds. The lowest rings will be 7cm from the bottom or from where the frill's seam is.

Sew on the heading tape to the wrong side of the blind before threading through the cords, and gather the tape up to fit the width of the blind.

3 Beds and bedding

This chapter contains some of the least complicated projects in the book – and some of the most difficult and most lavish. If you are completely new to sewing or soft furnishing, you may gain confidence and enthusiasm by starting off with an ordinary pillowcase in a fabric to match your bedroom; or you could tackle a simple throw-over bedspread or a duvet cover. The other bedspreads and even some of the bed hangings are not as difficult as they appear, but it would be best to leave the corona and drapes until you have mastered the basic techniques.

The savings in making sheets and pillowcases are not great but your bed may be an unusual size or you may want to choose your own fabric in a particular colour or pattern. Pillowcases can look attractive in the same patterned material as the sheets or duvet cover. Cotton or a cotton/polyester mix are the fabrics generally used and you can, of course, add decorative borders, frills or lace edgings. Making them up is relatively easy.

As a postscript we have included instructions for making curtains for a dressing-table, something that you may want to bring into your bedroom's decorating scheme.

BED LINEN

Sheets

First determine the width of fabric you need. Sheeting comes in a width of 228cm which is generally wide enough to avoid uncomfortable seams.

Measure across the bed and add double the depth of the mattress. Add 45cm for each side as a tuck-under. For the length, measure the length of the bed, plus twice the depth of the mattress, plus 30cm for the head end, and 45cm for a tuck-under at the bottom. Add an allowance for a double 7.5cm hem at the top, and a double 5cm hem at the bottom.

Cut out the material and machine-sew both the hems. Repeat for a pair. You could give the top sheet a decorative lace or broderie anglaise edging.

Fitted sheets

The elasticated fitting is used on all four corners of the sheet to pull it taut. This is where you can really benefit from doing the work yourself by achieving a perfect fit for your particular bed.

3.1a and b   Fitted sheets: [a] Stitch the corners of the basic shape. [b] Insert elastic to fit

Measure the length and width of the mattress. Add to these measurements twice the depth of the mattress. Add 11.5cm to each side and end to allow for the part tucked underneath the mattress (10cm) and for hem allowances of 1.5cm. Buy sheeting to these measurements and a metre of 1cm wide elastic. Cut out the fabric.

Mark in pins at all the corners a square with sides measuring the mattress depth plus 10cm. Cut out and machine-stitch the corners, right sides together. Trim off the excess fabric and neaten the edges, which is best done by machine-zigzagging [**3.1a**].

Press up a hem on the wrong side all the way round the sheet, taking 5mm on the first turning and 2cm on the second. Machine-stitch along all four sides but start and finish 15cm from the corners. Also stitch round the corners but leave 2cm gaps to insert the elastic [**3.1b**]. Cut the elastic into four lengths of 25cm each. Insert one into each corner with a bodkin and stitch the ends level with the openings so that the corners are gathered up.

Plain pillowcase

The pillowcase has a pocket or 'housewife' which holds the pillow in position. You can make the case from one, two or three sections, depending on whether you are making the case from small pieces or a generous length. Not all manufactured pillows come in a standard size so you will need to measure your pillow. For a one-piece case, measure the length and width of the pillow. The fabric should be the width of the pillow plus 8cm for turnings, and room for getting the pillow in and out easily. The length should be twice the length of the pillow plus 23cm for the pocket, turnings and room for manoeuvre. Try to cut the piece so that one of the short ends has a selvedge.

Press under the opposite end by 6.5cm and stitch under 5mm of that, close to the edge, to make a double hem. Fold the selvedge end over, wrong sides together, to make a pocket 15cm long, and over that fold up the hemmed end. Also wrong sides together, stitch the side edges half a centimetre in from the edge, and trim the seams to half that. Turn the pillowcase wrong side out and press the seams. Stitch again, 5mm in from the edge to form a French seam. Turn and press the finished pillowcase.

If you cut the fabric in two or three sections, the seams must fall where the fabric folds over to make the housewife pocket, and/or at the other end. Join the sections with French seams. Continue as for the one-piece pillowcase.

Pillowcase with frill

A frill adds a decorative touch to a pillow and is popular when used with a duvet since the pillows are visible during the day. This type of pillowcase is made from three sections, plus the frill. The separate pocket section should be cut to the width of the top and bottom sections and to a depth of 16cm.

Start by making the frill itself. Its length will be 1½ to 2 times the perimeter of the pillow. You may find it convenient to economise on cutting by making up the frill from shorter widths. Seams do not matter as they will be unobtrusive. Sew the widths end to end, open out the seams and press them. The width of the frill itself should be a doubled 2.5cm, plus 2.5cm for the seam, so a total of 7.5cm.

Sew the short ends of the long strip together, right sides together, and open and press them. Fold the fabric lengthwise, wrong sides together, into a continuous tube, and sew two lines of gathering stitch all round, 1.25cm and 1cm in from the raw edges.

Gather up the frill to the outer dimensions of the case. Pin it to one of the main sections, right sides and raw edges together. Adjust the frill to give a fairly even gather all round except on the corners, where it is important to have plenty of fullness or the finished frill will not stand out well from the pillow.

Sew the frill round the pillow along the line of the gathering stitch nearest to the edge of the frill. Take the pocket section and make it a double hem down one of its lengths, allowing 18mm for turnings. Lay it over the frilled section of the pillowcase, right sides together, and sew along the end seam [**3.2**]. Press it right sides out.

Make a double hem across one end of the other section with 18mm turnings. Place the two pieces of fabric right sides together, and stitch round the sides and bottom 1cm in from the raw edges. Keep the frill carefully tucked in so that you do not catch it in the seams. You cannot use a French seam if you are inserting a frill so you will

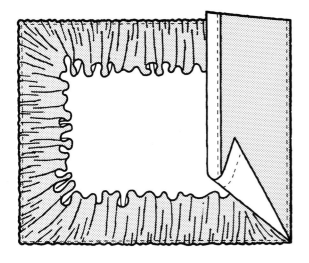

3.2   Attaching the frill and pocket to a frilled pillowcase

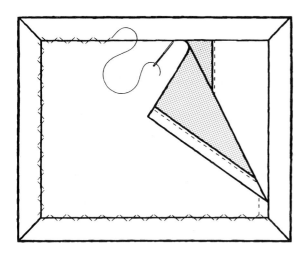

3.3   Assembling a bordered pillowcase

have to trim the corners and neaten the seams with machine-zigzagging, or overcasting by hand.

Bordered pillowcase

Again, you will have to make this type of pillow-case from three pieces of material (four, if the border is contrasting). The bottom piece should be the width and length of the pillow plus 8cm for turnings, and room for getting the pillow in and out. The top should have an extra 14cm added to the width and length which allows for borders of 6cm and a total of 2cm of turnings. The pocket section should be the width of the bottom section and 16cm deep.

First machine-sew a narrow hem along one of the short ends of the bottom piece, then along one of the long ends of the pocket.

Fold under all the edges of the larger top piece by 1cm and press down another 7cm. Mitre the corners and sew down the mitring to form a neat border. Take the pocket piece and, with wrong sides together, slip the raw edges between the folded border at one end. Tack it and then machine-zigzag (or sew by hand) only along the long edge.

Now place the prepared bottom section on the top piece, wrong sides together, so that the hem is at the pocket end. Insert all the raw edges evenly between the border. Tack them in position and zigzag stitch to finish. All the raw edges are thus hidden within the border [3.3].

If you want the border to be in a contrasting material cut four strips the length of the pillow plus twice the depth of the border, plus 1cm for two 1cm turnings. Each piece should be about 14cm wide (which will give a border of 6cm plus a total of 2cm for turnings). The top and bottom sections of the case will have the same dimensions this time.

Fold the strips in half lengthwise, and mitre and stitch the corners, right sides together. Turn and press the border, and slip it between the pre-pared main sections of the pillowcase (again you will have to use three pieces of fabric in order to accommodate the border). The inside edges of this version will be raw so you should machine-zigzag them or overcast them by hand.

Instead of fabric strips you could use lengths of ruched lace and slip a single layer of it between the top and bottom of the pillowcase.

DUVET

You may think it worthwhile to make your own duvet only if you have an unusually large bed. Alternatively, you may want to convert an old eiderdown but you will have to supplement the filling as an equivalent duvet needs more down.

The duvet consists of a channelled bag filled with goose or duck down, feathers or synthetic material. Goose down is considered the best and most luxurious because it is the lightest, but synthetic filling is the cheapest, easiest to handle and is washable. The bag is divided into compartments to keep the feathers evenly distributed. Its light weight and flexibility enable it to sink around the sleeper's body, eliminating pockets of cold air and providing perfect insulation.

You can buy the type of filling you prefer from a good upholstery supplier. The fabric used for the duvet itself must be a downproof cambric which is waxed on one side to stop the sharp quills poking through. The cambric is covered by a second bag which is taken off for washing.

To decide upon the size of the duvet, measure the bed from top to bottom and from side to side. Add at least 20cm at the bottom of the bed for the overhang, and at least 40cm to the width measurement for the overhang at the two sides. It relies on its weight to seal up the gaps at the side of the bed and if you have insufficient overhang, you may well find that the edges are not sealed. To all these measurements add a further 2.5cm at the top, bottom and both sides for the seam turnings. Cut two pieces of cambric to these measurements.

Sew them with French seams around the two sides and top. If the cambric is too small to make the bag from one width, sew widths together using a French seam, joining right sides (unwaxed) together first. Trim the seam turnings, turn the bag inside out and machine-sew round the seams again.

Divide the bag into tubes of an equal width as near to 20cm wide as possible, running lengthwise down the bag. Mark the sewing lines with chalk and sew down them [3.4a]. The bulk may present some problems to your sewing-machine, but if you sew from each side towards the centre, folding the remainder of the fabric into a neat roll as you go, you should be able to cope. A

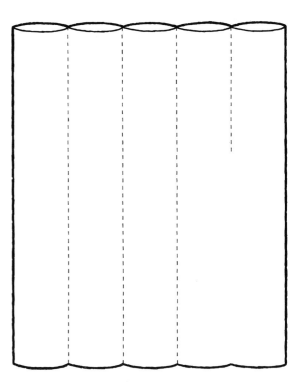

3.4a and b   Duvet: [a] Divide the bag into equal channels. [b] Keep the filled channels sealed with clothes pegs while filling

refinement, if you are going to fill the duvet with feathers, would be to wax down the stitching with a piece of beeswax to prevent the quills poking up through the sewing holes.

You can now fill the tubes. You need enough to stop most of the heat loss from your body but you will defeat the object if you pack the tubes so tightly that they become stiff and inflexible. One tube of average length will take about 250g of filling.

Down and feathers are unruly objects to have flying about so you might find it preferable to carry out the filling operation in the garden on a still day. A washing line is a useful accessory. Peg the duvet case at the seams along the washing line so that you can use both hands while the openings at the top of the tubes stay open. Divide the filling into as many portions as there are tubes, each weighing about 250g. Contain them temporarily in large polythene bags closed with pegs.

Take one bag, plunge your hand in, take a firm handful of filling or feathers and stuff it right down into the first tube before you release it.

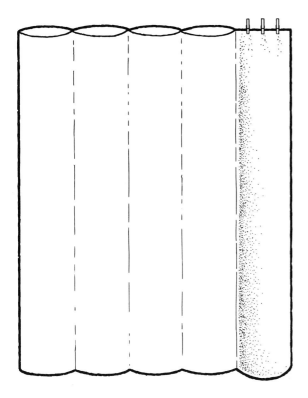

That way you should be able to keep losses to a minimum.

When you have used up the bagful, close off the opening to the tube with a peg or two, and go on to the next [**3.4b**]. When you have distributed the filling and have a nicely fat duvet without any stiffness, and all the holes are closed off with pegs, take the duvet down from the washing line, tack and sew (and wax) the last seam. You could enclose the raw edges with bias binding to neaten them.

Duvet cover
By comparison, making an outer cover for the duvet is simple. Buy polyester/cotton sheeting (which comes in extra-wide widths) as large as the duvet, adding a 10cm margin to both the width and length to avoid restricting the duvet it-self. Sew it round the top and two sides making a French seam. Turn in the allowance at the bottom edge into a double 2cm seam, stitch up about 10cm at each side and attach 'poppered' tape or Velcro to close the opening.

COT LINING

Washable and reversible cotton/polyester quilting is by far the best material for lining a cot as its padding will prevent the baby hurting itself against the cot bars, and it will keep out draughts.

You will need fabric to go round the four sides of the cot but it need not go right up to the top of the bars – about 30cm high is easily enough to protect a baby's head. The base of the cot lining goes under the mattress so it can be made from lining material, calico or other washable left-over fabric. You will also need 2.5m of ribbon to match the quilting.

Cut the fabric for the four sides and the base, including seam allowances of 1.25cm [**3.5**]. Join the two short ends to one of the long sides so that the right side of the seams will face in towards the cot. Trim the seams, press them and cover them with binding to neaten them. Also bind the raw edges of the two end pieces and round the top edge.

Sew the base to these three sides, right side of quilting to under side of the base – all the raw edges will eventually be hidden by the mattress. Turn the structure so that the seams are inside.

Then deal with the remaining long side, first binding its side and top edges and then sewing it to the open edge of the base, wrong sides together. The fourth side has to be unattached, except at the base, so that when the side of the cot is let down it doesn't get in the way.

Cut the ribbon into 12 equal lengths (about 20cm long) and attach six in three pairs down each long side of the cot lining – at each corner and at or near the middle to correspond with a cot bar. The ribbons are tied round the bars to keep the lining in place.

3.5   Construction of a cot lining

54

BEDSPREADS AND VALANCES

The traditional bedspread offers an almost limit-less range of design possibilities. The instructions here cover a variety of types from a simple throw-over bedspread to more complicated fitted styles. By adapting them you will be able to achieve exactly the effect you want, whether you are designing your bedspread or copying one from a magazine or shop display [3.6].

A valance covers the base of the bed when a duvet or a half-length throw-over bedspread is used. It can be made from the same material as the sheets and duvet cover, probably polyester/cotton sheeting in the same or a contrasting colour, or a heavier fabric. The part of the valance that covers the base of the bed under the mattress is never seen, so it can be made from lining fabric, calico, or a piece of old sheeting as long as it is not worn. If it stretched out right to the sides of the bed it might just be visible between the mattress and the base, so it is surrounded by a narrow border in the same fabric as the sides.

There are various styles: a simple gathered frill, box-pleats, or kick pleats at the corners of a straight-sided valance. It can go all round the bed, or just round the sides and bottom if the head of the bed is against a wall.

Throw-over bedspread

One of the simplest and most effective bed-spreads consists of a piece of fabric cut to size, sewn, and draped over the bed, almost touching the floor. If you want to have a valance round the base of the bed, the cover can hang to just below the top of the valance.

If you want to take the bedspread off the bed at night, any weight of fabric is suitable though a washable and crease-resistant one would be best. A plain or printed linen, cotton or synthetic fabric would be the cheapest. Brocades and satins produce luxurious results but if you are new to sewing it would be wise to avoid these expensive materials. Otherwise, the finest fabric you can afford is well invested in a bedspread. Cotton lace comes in very wide widths so you don't have to join any seams. If you intend to use the spread as part of the bedclothes, washable quilted fabric would be a good choice since it is particularly crease-resistant and very warm.

3.6   A range of bedspreads

Measuring the bed

Start by measuring the bed. Make up the bed with the usual bedclothes and pillows in place.

Using a fabric tape, measure the width over the bed from the floor one side to the floor the other. Add 20cm to give a double 5cm hem at each side, and 5cm for each seam. Subtract 2cm from the total to give a 1cm clearance at each side, just enough to stop the bedspread brushing the floor. If you are making a half-spread for use with a valance, measure over the made-up bed down to a point 10cm below the bottom of the mattress.

Measuring the length, start at the head of the bed and measure along the length down to the floor at the foot (or to 10cm below the bottom of the mattress). Add 10cm for a double 5cm hem there, plus 18cm to tuck down behind the head end of the bed, and a further 5cm for a double 2.5cm turning at the top. The measurements are slightly flexible in that the depth of the hemming is not critical all round and no attempt is made to accommodate the bulk of the pillows. You will find that this simple design of bedspread falls neatly, even if a little way off the floor at each side near the head end.

Estimating the fabric

All beds take more than one width of fabric. A single bed, say 75cm wide and 37.5cm high, would require a 150cm width of material plus hem and seam allowances. This would come comfortably from two widths of most fabrics, so you would need to buy fabric amounting to twice the total length. If you choose a material with a large pattern, allow extra for matching, about the depth of one pattern repeat for each width.

For a large double bed, perhaps 135cm wide and 67.5cm off the floor, the total width of fabric would need to be 270cm, plus hem and seam allowances. Clearly you could not form this from two widths of fabric, even using a wide weave of 135cm, so you would have to buy three times the length measurement. Unfortunately, this involves a lot of waste.

Whether you are making a single or a double bedspread it is important to have a complete panel down the centre of the bed with seams to either side, avoiding an unsightly centre join. Cut across the width to the required length, starting each piece from the same point in the pattern if

3.7a, b and c Bedspread with rounded corners: [a] Mark the curve with pins. [b] Fold and use the first corner as a cutting guide for the second. [c] Make a double hem

3.8a, b and c Bedspread with slit corners: [a] Mark a
square. [b] Cut and bind the square. [c] Hand-stitch the
binding to the wrong side

the material has an obvious repeat. For a single
bedspread, fold the material in half lengthwise
and cut along the fold. Cut one of the pieces in
half along its length. The halves will be sewn to
the sides of the full centre panel width. You may
need to reduce the width of this centre section so
that the seams fall in appropriate places – i.e. not
down the vertical sides.

Making up the cover
Join the lengths, right sides together, using a flat
seam with a 2cm allowance. Cut the selvedge off
if the fabric is glazed chintz. Otherwise, make
notches along the selvedges at 15cm intervals to
prevent any puckering. Press the seams open and
neaten the raw edges by machine-zigzagging or
hand overcasting. Alternatively, you could use a
run-and-fell seam.

There are two choices for the treatment of corners. If you sew the hems all round as they are,
mitring the corners, you will find that there is a
great flap of excess. This is acceptable but you
may prefer to avoid the corners trailing by trimming the fabric to meet the floor.

To form the cutting line for rounded corners,
lay the bedspread fabric on the bed. Take hold of
the fabric at one of the bottom corners and ease it
down to the point where it meets the floor. Mark
this point with a pin. Continue marking with a
pin round the fabric from one side to the other

until you have a curved line of pins all round the
excess fabric. Trim the fabric to the line of the
curve [3.7a]. To cut the other side, fold the fabric
in half and follow the first cutting line [3.7b]. The
bedspread will now fit to the floor neatly on both
sides of the bed.

Turn in and press 2.5cm all round the bedspread. If you are making rounded corners, stitch
close to the foldline and pleat or notch the allowance to take up the excess fabric [3.7c]. Fold the
material over again to form a double hem. Mitre
the corners at the top of the bed.

The bedspread is now finished. It should tuck
neatly down behind the pillows at the top and
hang comfortably just off the floor or over the top
of the valance all round.

If the bed has posts or a foot rail you will need
to make slit corners [3.8a, b and c]. When you
have joined the panels together, lay the cover on
the bed and pin the corner. Remove the cover and
cut out a square, leaving a 1cm seam allowance.
Cut a bias strip of the main fabric, sew it to the
cover, right sides together, and clip the curves as
you turn it under. Hand-stitch the remaining
edge to the wrong side of the cover.

If the bed has a solid board at the foot, measure
the length of the top panel so that there is an
allowance for tucking down between the mattress
and the board. The bottom corners will be
mitred.

Lined throw-over bedspread

The advantages of lining a bedspread are warmth (especially if you use a quilted lining) and a neater, crease-resistant finish. Use a lining fabric that is compatible in terms of washing or dry-cleaning with the main fabric. Cut it out and sew the seams exactly as for the main cover. With wrong sides together, lockstitch the cover and lining together along the seams. Turn in the lining, tack it to the bedspread 2.5cm in from the edge all round and slip stitch it into position.

An alternative method would be to place the lining and cover right sides together and machine-stitch all round the edge leaving a 60cm gap along the top edge. Trim square corners diagonally and pleat or notch round corners. Turn the bedspread right side out and press it. Slip stitch the opening together.

Throw-over bedspread with pillow flap

If you use one or even two large pillows, their bulk can throw the line of the bedspread out of balance unless some provision is made for it. One simple solution is to add a flap (or 'scarf') to the top of the bedspread. The cover itself lies flat under the pillows but the flap returns over them and then tucks underneath [3.9b].

If the bedspread were made from a single piece of fabric, the part showing over the pillows would be the wrong side of the fabric, so the flap is cut separately and sewn on in reverse [3.9a].

Measure the length of the bed, without pillows, from the head of the bed to the floor, remembering the hem allowances. Replace the pillows and measure loosely from the top of the bed, over the pillows and back under them for about 20cm, to determine the length of the extra flap. The flap should be wide enough at least to cover the pillows or even to reach the floor on each side, so that it hangs in an attractive fold. Take care when you cut the fabric that any prominent design is centrally placed. Sew the flap to the main part of the cover, wrong side of the flap to right side of the bedspread. Sew a double hem all round the flap.

If you are going to line the bedspread you will have to line the main panel and the flap separately, and then join the two elements by a run-and-fell seam so that all the edges are neatly enclosed.

3.9a and b Bedspread with pillow flap: [a] Cut the flap separately. [b] The flap returns and tucks underneath the pillow

Throw-over bedspread with pillow gusset

An alternative way of accommodating the pillows is to sew a gusset into the side of the bedspread. The bedspread will then fit neatly over the bed and pillows together. If you have a gusset, the rest of the design is usually tailored to the bed's dimensions too and incorporates piping into all the seams. The sides can be gathered, plain with kick-pleats at the bottom corners, or box-pleated.

You will have to estimate the shape of the gusset to fit the pillows. A useful measurement that would accommodate most single pillows is 12cm high and 40cm long, rising in a generous curve to match the curve of the pillow. The dimensions can be increased for two pillows or one very full one. Add a 2.5cm seam allowance round the curve, and 5cm seam allowances along the straight bottom and at the end hem. You may find it helpful to make a paper pattern of the area before you cut the material. Remember to cut one left-hand and one right-hand gusset.

When you are measuring for the top panel of the cover add on 25 or 30cm to allow for the height of the pillows and for a little to tuck behind them. If you are not lining the bedspread make all seams 5cm wide to allow for neatening; otherwise they can be 2.5cm wide. The measurements for the frill, straight or box-pleated sides will be from the top of the mattress (with normal bedclothes in position) down to 1cm above the floor, plus 5cm for the hem and 1cm for the seam at the top.

Prepare the sides first. Then deal with the gusset. If you are using interlining, tack or iron it to the wrong side of the gusset and press the seam allowances, especially round the curved part of the gusset. Turn in and sew the 5cm end allowance into a 2.5cm double hem.

You will need enough piping to go right round the side and bottom edges of the bed and along the curved part of the gusset (see page 80 for how to make it). First sew a short length of piping to the bottom straight edge of the gusset [3.10a]. Then sew the gusset to the skirt of the bedspread, right side to right side [3.10b], and turn over the seam allowance to tidy up the raw edges. Next sew piping to the curved part of the gusset and continue this piping right round the skirt of the bedspread. The piping of the curved part of the gusset should lie over the piping of the lower straight edge for a neater finish [3.10c].

Lastly, you can machine the skirt and gusset to the top panel of the bedspread. Clip the curves, particularly round the top of the gusset.

If you want to line a fitted cover, cut a lining for the top panel, gussets and sides. Assemble the pieces and apply the lining to the cover wrong side to wrong side. If it is a full lining, lockstitch along the seams, turn and press under all the raw

3.10a, b and c Throw-over bedspread with pillow gusset: [a] Sew piping to the base of the gusset. [b] Sew the gusset to the skirt. [c] Make a neat finish with the piping

edges of the lining, tack them to the cover and hem them in position. Otherwise, turn in and press the half-lining (one that lines the top panel only) and sew it down over the seams of the cover to hide them.

If you are not lining the cover, double-hem the top edge of the main panel and hem round the frill or the sides.

3.11a and b   Frilled valance: [a] Tack the frill to the base panel. [b] Add piping

Frilled valance

The instructions given are for a three-sided valance. Measure the length and width of the base of the bed. The base panel will have these measurements plus 4cm for turnings, plus an extra 25cm for a large flap to tuck in at the top.

The valance is made from a long gathered strip of fabric to go round the sides and bottom of the bed. Measure the depth of the base from its top to the floor. Add 2cm for the seam allowance at the top, and 4cm for a double 2cm hem at the bottom. Subtract 1cm for clearance off the floor. This measurement is the height of the frill. To look right, the pattern must run vertically so you should cut the strips from several widths of the fabric joined together. Measure the length of the bed, double it to allow for the two sides, and add the width of the bed. Double this total to accommodate the gather. You can now calculate how many widths you will have to cut and join.

For the three borders cut three strips of the same fabric as the frill, each about 20cm wide (15cm plus two seam allowances of 2.5cm), two the length and one the width of the mattress (each plus 2.5cm for turnings).

Tack the wrong side of the border lengths to the right side of the bottom panel, outer edges together, press under 2.5cm on the inside edges of the border, mitring the corners, and then machine round.

Sew together the lengths of fabric for the frill. Press the seams open and neaten the edges. Mark a sewing line 1.5cm from the top edge all along the strip. Double the length of the bed and mark off this measurement from one end of the strip with a tailor's tack. Then double the width of the bed and mark off that position from the first mark. These are the positions of the corners at the bottom of the bed. Turn up and stitch a double 2cm hem all the way round, and hem what will be the vertical ends of the frill.

Gather along the sewing line as far as the first mark. Repeat along the part marked for the width, then along the final length. Sew a second row of gathering along the same lengths, the width of the sewing-machine foot (about 25mm if you are hand-sewing) away from the first line, nearer the edge.

Gather up one side of the frill as far as the first tailor's tack. Draw the threads up until the side is as long as the bed and wind them securely round a pin. Match the position of the pin on the frill to the corner of the base fabric. Tack and then sew the frill and the base panel together, right sides together, with a 2cm seam allowance [**3.11a**]. (The beginning of the frill should start 25cm from the top end of the lining fabric where the flap at the head of the bed will be.) Add piping at this stage [**3.11b**]. Next draw up the gathers and sew the bottom of the valance, and finally the third side, again, as far as a point 25cm from the end. Grade the seams and neaten the edges. Turn in and slip stitch the unsewn ends of the border, and hem round the flap.

You can now fit the valance to the bed. If you wish, you can slip stitch the sides of the flap to the vertical ends of the frill so that the cover does not get dislodged. You can also sew on tapes to tie round the inner sides of the bed legs to ensure that the valance stays in place.

Valance with straight sides and kick-pleats, or with box-pleats

Make the valance as if you were constructing the flat fitted bedspread in either of its variations described next in the chapter. Measure the depth of the side panels or pleats from the top of the mattress base. Instructions for the base panel under the mattress are as for the frilled valance. You will probably want to pipe the edges round the mattress base in keeping with the more tailored line of the pleats or kick-pleats.

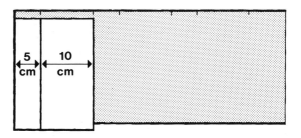

Flat fitted bedspread or divan cover with box-pleat valance

This cover is particularly suitable for bed-sit or studio beds which turn into sofas during the day. It would be sensible to choose quite a heavy and hard-wearing fabric with a firm weave such as a heavy cotton/polyester mix or furnishing tweed.

For the top centre panel measure to the edges, allowing about 1cm for the side and bottom seams and 23cm for an 18cm pillow tuck with a double 2.5cm hem at the top. Join widths of fabric as necessary to make up the total width.

Place a saucer at the bottom two corners and cut along the line of its curve in order to give the bedspread gently rounded corners.

The depth of the valance will be as for a frilled valance, in other words from the base of the mattress to 1cm above the floor. Add on 2.5cm for the hem and just over 1cm for the top turning. You will have to join strips of fabric (attached so that the straight grain on all pieces runs vertically) to a length that is three times the total length of the two sides and bottom of the centre panel, plus 2.5cm for turnings. You may want the valance to go right round the bed, in which case you should adjust the total measurement accordingly.

Turn up and press the hem of the valance before you form the pleats. Pleats of about 10cm width are usual, but their actual width will be dictated by the length of the edge of the bed. Divide that length into equal pleats as near as possible to 10cm wide. This way the ends of the pleats will occur neatly at the corners.

Make a cardboard template to form accurate pleats. It should be the exact width and depth of the pleat you want [3.12a]. Lay the joined strips of fabric out flat, wrong side up and, using the template, mark with chalk or pins the position of

3.12a and b Box-pleated valance: [a] Plan the pleats. [b] Construct the folds

the pleats all the way along. Fold the pleats as in [3.12b]. Seams in the strip must be hidden in the folds of the pleats. Tack the pleats in position. Sew any piping to the centre panel and attach the valance to it. Neaten the seam or slip stitch the edges of the centre panel's lining down over the seam.

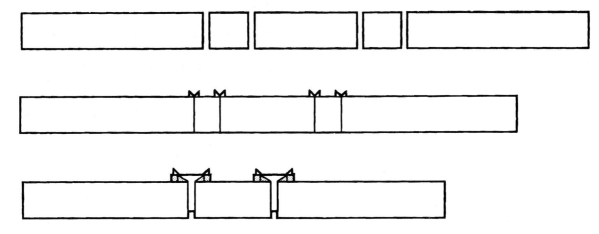

3.13a, b and c Straight sides and kick-pleats: [a] Lay out the panels. [b] Stitch with flat seams. [c] Form the kick-pleats

Flat fitted bedspread or divan cover with straight sides and kick-pleats

This is another tailored variation for a cover, using less material than the box-pleated one. Again, you should choose a fairly hard-wearing fabric.

Follow the instructions for making the centre panel as given for the box-pleated version, gently rounding the corners. Cut two panels for the sides the length of the centre panel, plus 30cm. Cut one panel for the bottom end the width of the bed, also plus 30cm. The depth of these three panels should be from the top of the mattress down to 1cm above the floor, plus 5cm for the hem and 1cm for the top seam allowance.

Cut two pieces of fabric on the straight grain 30cm long and the same depth as the side panels. Join up the sides and end, using a normal flat seam and right sides together, in this order: side panel, corner pleat, end panel, corner pleat, side panel. Take up a double 2.5cm hem all round.

Bring the seams together for each corner so that the corner pleat sections are hidden. Make sure that each side of the pleat is an equal 14cm. Attach any piping to the top panel. Then position the valance to it so that the pleats fall precisely at the corners. Tack and sew the seams, and neaten them if you are not lining the bedspread. Hem along the top ends of the centre panel and the valance where there is the small allowance (about 18cm) for tucking behind the pillows. Line the centre panel if you want (the valance need not be lined), hemming the edges over the main seams to neaten them.

If you want to make a valance that goes right round the bed with four kick-pleats, [**3.13a, b and c**], the measurement for the side panels will be the same because the 15cm that in the three-sided version tucks behind the pillows will go instead towards the kick-pleat there. The centre panel will have the measurements of the bed plus 1cm seam allowances all round.

One-piece box cover

This is a variation on the flat fitted bedspread but makes the sofa look even less bed-like during the day. Take the measurements for the cover over the usual bedclothes but without the pillows, following the guidelines given previously, depending on whether you want a frill, box-pleats or straight sides with kick-pleats, but take into account the fact that the valance goes round all four sides of the bed.

The new element in this design is the straight band round the sides of the mattress. Form this from strips of fabric (as few as possible) the depth of the mattress plus two 2cm turnings. If you want to pipe the edges tack piping all the way round the top panel. Lay the panel upside down on the mattress and pin the band to the piped edge. Join the two ends of the band at a corner and try to contrive that other joins will occur at points where the divan is against a wall. Stitch and press the seam open. Line the centre panel.

Tack piping to the lower edge of the band. Form the valance and turn up its hem. Lay the piped lower edge of the band over the tacked pleats or gathers and stitch along at the base of the piping through all layers. Neaten the seams.

Decorative borders

A border in a contrasting fabric is an easy way to add unusual interest to the bedspread. You could position a border down each side of the bed from the head to the foot, or place one border on one side of the bed only. Classical in style, and fitted by cutting to a mitred shape at the corners, is a border which follows the outline of the bed: fit it about 20cm from the sides and end of the bed all round. Borders must be cut on the straight grain of the fabric, turned under and pressed evenly, then sewn on to the cover by machine or hemmed invisibly by hand. Apply any decorative border before you line the bedspread.

Patchworked and quilted bedspreads

Traditionally there are favourite techniques in bedspread-making because of their combined economic, decorative and insulating properties.

If you want to make a quilted bedspread, whether or not with patchwork, make the simplest sort – the throw-over cover either full or half-length – as this will show off the work best.

HEADBOARDS

Headboards come in a wide variety of shapes, fabrics and forms, and should be an integral part of the design of the bed and the bedroom.

The instructions here cover the woodwork needed to make up a headboard, padding and covering it, and making loose covers of various kinds. Take up the instructions at the point where they apply to your particular needs.

Designing the headboard

First, design your headboard and examine the fixing system by which it is to be applied to your bed. A typical system involves two screw-headed bolts, with large diameter washers, over which you place slotted lengths of wood. The headboard itself is screwed to the wood.

Make sure you have enough wood above the mattress to support the headboard itself. The dimensions of the board depend on the design. Normally it will be the width of the bed but some designs incorporate small drawers and tables at the sides. However, it is not wise to put all that weight of furniture and contents on just the two bolts screwed into the bed. Instead, there is another alternative. That is to fix the headboard to the wall, and push the bed up against it. For that you will need to arrange a fixing system. It may be a simple screw into a plugged hole in the wall, in which case you will have to leave access space for the screw head before you finally fit the padding and covering fabric. Or you may be able to buy a spike and sleeve system at a hardware shop to slot the headboard on to the wall and take it off when you need to.

Sit on the bed comfortably and find out where your head touches the wall when you are reading, drinking tea, or watching the midnight movie. Design the headboard to end several centimetres higher than this (maybe even 20cm). You can have a straight or shaped top edge. Draw the design on to 5-ply or chipboard, perhaps with the aid of a paper pattern, and cut round it. Cover the board completely with 2.5cm thick foam cut to the shape and glued on (you could use the paper pattern again).

You may want to take the foam over the top and round the edges. If so, cut out the corners to avoid a bulky overlap.

3.14a and b Deep-buttoned headboard: [a] Tacks hammered halfway. [b] Thread passed through the button and wound round the tack

Padding and covering the headboard

If you are making a board with a permanent cover you may like to consider a button arrangement, whether a pattern of deep- buttoning as on a Victorian chair, or a single button in the centre of the headboard.

Plot the button design in the early stages and drill a small hole through the board at each intended button point. At the back of the board, hammer halfway in a small tack close to the hole [**3.14a**]. Later, whichever type of button you fit, you can push a needle through the hole, the foam and the fabric, thread on a button, push the needle back through, draw the thread tight and wrap it round the tack [**3.14b**], before hammering home the tack for a permanent fixing.

With the foam glued in place, you can deal with the fabric. Cut it to the shape of the board with a generous overlap all round, centring any patterns. Tauten the fabric over the board and secure it with upholsterer's tacks between the wooden fixing struts at the bottom of the board. Smooth it out towards one side without pulling it too tight, and secure that side with more tacks. Repeat the other side. At the corners, draw the fabric up into a flap and tack it down. Trim off the excess fabric. At the bottom, where the struts

hold the board, you will need to cut the fabric into the corners, and fold it away to conceal the raw edge. Tack the fabric down securely. Fit buttons, if required, at this stage.

For a professional finish you could line the back. Fold the edges under neatly, and hammer in tacks all round at 2cm–3cm intervals. As an alternative you could back the board with fabric lining. Fold the edge under and slip stitch the lining to the facing fabric all round.

Another permanent design would be to cut the foam to fit the exact shape of the board without taking it over the edge to the back. Cut the facing fabric to exactly the same size plus 1cm all round for seam allowances, and then cut a strip wide enough to match the thickness of the foam plus that of the board, also plus 1cm for seam allowances.

Make up piping in a matching or contrasting colour and sandwich it between the two parts. You could make the back in the same fabric, add a second line of piping, or finish the back in lining fabric for economy.

A few tacks hammered into the lining fabric just below the top edge of the board will help to prevent the whole assembly pulling forwards in use, revealing the lining fabric at the back.

64

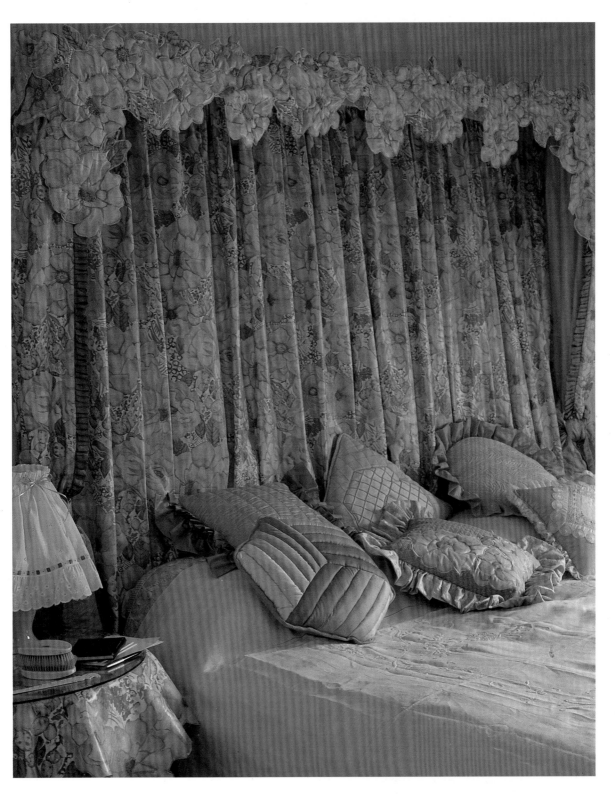

Many soft furnishings projects are incorporated in
this bedroom setting: canopied bed, matching tablecloth, a variety of cushions with decorative edgings
and a simple broderie anglaise lampshade.

Above left: these quilted bed covers in a simple diamond pattern are shown to their best effect by using a plain material.

Above right: appliquéd quilt and frilled pillows.

Left: the dramatic drapes for this four-poster bed have been created by using bold contrasting colours.

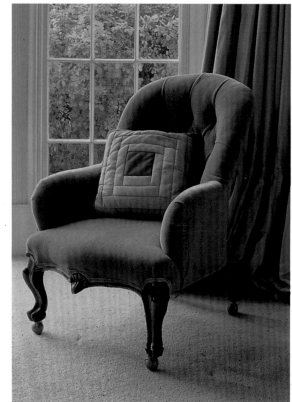

Above: a tablecloth made from patchwork hexagons.

Above right: a simple first project: a cushion using strips of green (logcabin patchwork).

Right: an easy and interesting use for nets – draped over bed poles for a very feminine finish.

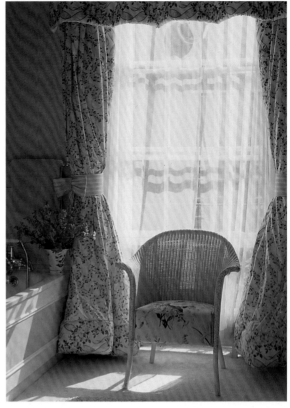

Above left: a daring room setting: a bold red print has been used for curtaining material and the same pattern for the wallpaper.

Above right: these bathroom curtains have padded hems. The tie-backs are created to resemble candy-striped bow-ties.

Left: a curtain-and-blind combination. The peach-coloured Austrian blinds are topped off with a short gathered valance, and floor-length curtains, held back with tie-backs, accentuate the height of the window.

Above: a sophisticated look is achieved with this mirror-set of two windows with matching swags and tails. The green curtains are lined in a lighter matching green and have fringing for further decoration.

Above left: the effect of lining a tail in a contrasting-coloured material can be seen in this illustration.

Above right: a swag with a simple knotted tail.

Left: a lined valance, trimmed with dark blue and finished with bows positioned at the head of the pleats.

Opposite: varieties of tie-backs; *top-left:* a fabric tie-back with contrasting backing; *top right:* tassel-cord tie-back; *bottom:* frilled tie-back.

Right: a frilled Austrian blind and a pretty deep-buttoned armchair, with gathered skirt and rosettes, are created from the same fabric. The panelled cushions incorporate a needlepoint design.

Left: a roman blind in bold green, yellow and white stripes. The sofa has been upholstered in a matching fabric.

Below: pretty floral-pink Austrian blinds let in the light; the effect is completed with matching full-length curtains hung at the side windows.

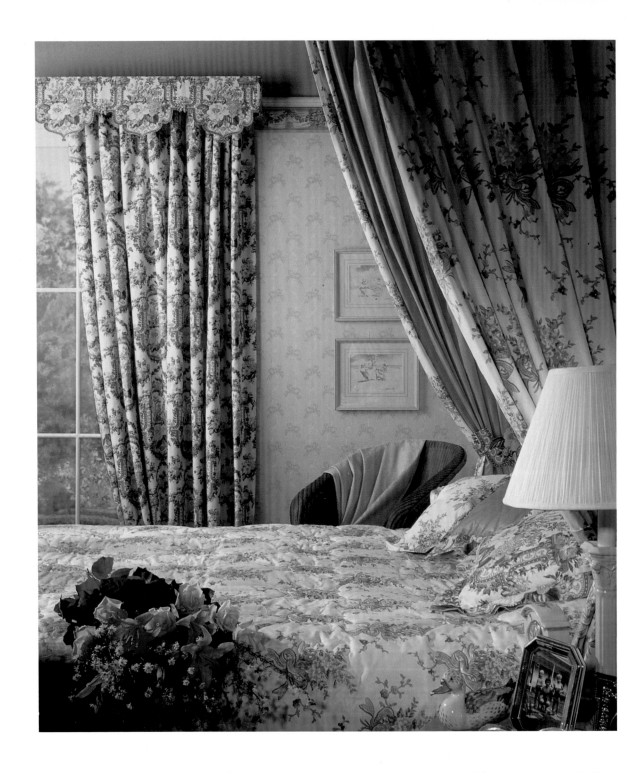

Another example of strong patterns being used throughout a room scheme. The shape of the pelmets has been dictated by the design of the material; the light-coloured fabric has also been used for the bed hangings, floor-length curtains and bordered pillows. A pale-coloured pleated lampshade provides the maximum of light.

Opposite top: a canopied four-poster bed with frilly valance. The effect is completed by matching floor-length curtains suspended from a pole.

Opposite bottom: two examples of skirted dressing-tables. To the right is a kidney-shaped dressing-table with a glass top (see page 68).

Above: a 'before-and-after' version of a re-covered sofa.

Left: a loose armchair cover with box pleats.

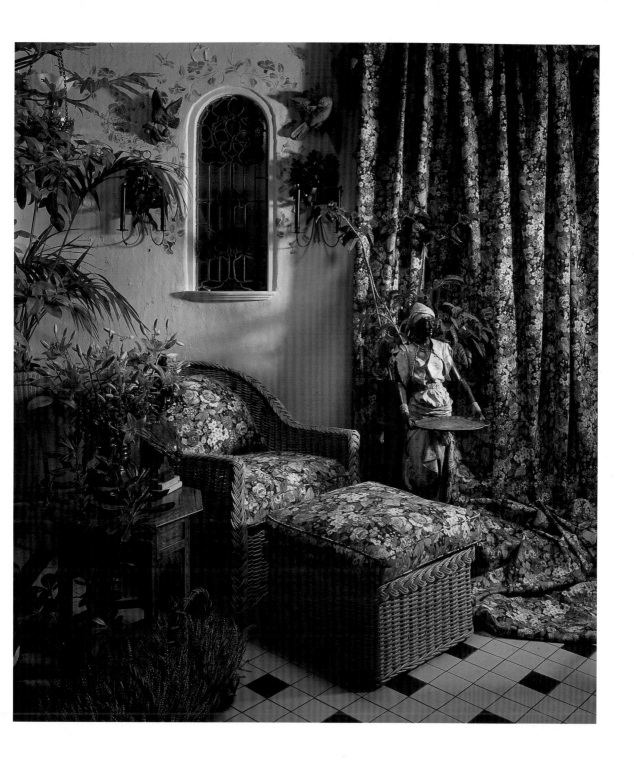

Curtains and piped cushions in a darker fabric create a very exotic mood.

Over: design ideas for cushions are limitless. *Above left:* an array of pink-quilted cushions; *above right:* lace-trimmed cushions; *below:* satin-effect cushions in rich colours complement the lighting in this sophisticated room.

Tablecloths: *top left:* throw-over tablecloth and squab cushions; *top right:* circular tablecloth with gathered pockets; *left:* quilted tablecloth and squab cushions with frills.

Previous page: Above: floral fabrics are used throughout this bedroom's design scheme; tails and swags; a covered stool and padded headboard.

Below left: bordered cushions are set against a plain-coloured canvas deck-chair.

Below right: a frilled valance on full curtains, pleated shades and a circular tablecloth.

Loose cover for a headboard

You may find it more practical to live with an easily laundered loose cover. Make the board as described but use a cheap backing fabric.

Quilted fabric with piped seams looks attractive and is very comfortable [3.15]. Cut the fabric and a lining for the back to the same dimensions as for the permanent cover. Remember to add on 1cm all round for the turnings. You will also need a gusset strip to fit round the top and sides (again, remember the seam allowances). Place this strip to the front piece, right sides together, inserting piping, and stitch. Trim the allowance to about 5mm, notch the curves and trim the corners. Join the back section in the same way [3.16].

If you do not want to make a gusset, you could trim the foam with scissors to make a smooth curve at the top so that the front and back sections can be joined to each other.

Along the open bottom end of the cover, turn up a double 6mm hem. Add tapes for tying the cover under the board at intervals of about 30cm to prevent it slipping around in use.

Wall-fixed bedhead

A cushion or a pair of box cushions attached to the wall is a particularly elegant arrangement if hung from a brass or wooden rod [3.17]. The cushions should hang to a point just above the top of the mattress. Make sure that the pole is high enough up the wall so you do not bang your head against it. The cushions should be stuffed with layers of synthetic wadding, or upholsterer's felt (linter's felt). Feathers or loose filling are not suitable because they will fall to the bottom of the cushion. Make the cushion into a pad, as thin or plump as you wish. Continue making the box cushions as described on page 95. Make the loops that will attach the cushions to the rod. Each loop will be about 40cm long and 10cm wide, but remember when cutting them out to allow for seam turnings. Follow the method for making curtain tabs. Sew the loops into the cushion casing to either side of the top gusset.

You can, of course, develop this idea by sewing decorative patterns on to the cushion front, or by making them up from quilting (page 14).

3.15   Loose cover for headboard

3.16   Attaching gusset and piping to the loose cover for the headboard

3.17   Pair of cushions forming a wall-fixed bedhead

BED HANGINGS

If you have a four-poster bed you may want to give it elaborate treatment with a frilled bed-spread or valance, but you will have to divide the cover and the frill at the bottom corners because of the posts. You may also want to make up a valance (or frill) to run round the top, or drapes round the posts, or even a fabric canopy to cover the roof.

All valances designed to hang round the top of a bed must be lined because they are seen from both sides. You should decide whether to line them in the same or in a contrasting fabric. You can bind either or both edges with contrasting bias binding. There are two methods of hanging the valances: either by sewing a casing through which the poles can be slotted, or, if the poles are not detachable, by affixing a standard curtain tape, as used for curtains.

Valance with a cased heading

Decide on the depth of the valance and add on the circumference of the pole and 2.5cm for turnings. Cut four strips of the main fabric all of this depth, two 1½ to 2 times the length of the side poles and two 1½ to 2 times the length of the end poles. Cut four equivalent lining strips. Make up the four valances separately by attaching the main fabric to the lining, right sides together, along the sides and bottom edge. Trim the corners, turn and press. Press in the top edges to the lining side by a centimetre or so, then turn them down again to a depth that will contain the pole snugly but without difficulty when the frill is ruched up. Tack along this line and then machine-stitch close to the lower edge of the casing. The pole can now be inserted into the casing [3.18].

If you want a small frill at the top of the casing, add on an extra centimetre to the depth of the four strips. Turn in the top edges of the facing fabric and the lining so that the raw edges are hidden between them, and slip stitch them together. Make two lines of stitching for the casing, the top one four or five centimetres down from the top, the other beneath it leaving enough room for the pole to slip in easily [3.19].

Valance with curtain tape

Measure the length of the valance as for those

3.18   Plain casing for a valance

3.19   Frilled casing for a valance

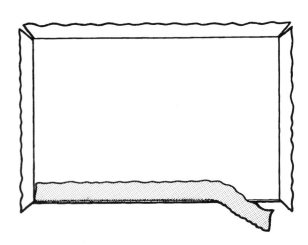

3.20   Construction of canopy with valances

with a cased heading but add 7.5cm for the top frill. Proceed as if you were making lined curtains. The finished valances can be hung by ordinary curtain hooks, or attached to curtain rings or screw eyes the length of the frame.

Canopies

Even more exotic or romantic hangings can be achieved with a canopy over the bed. The canopy is really a roof covering the whole of the bed and can be plain or ruched.

Make up four lined valances, joining the bottom and the sides. Make two rows of gathering along the top edges 2 and 2.5cm from the edge. Cut two pieces of fabric for the canopy the size of the rectangle formed by the poles, plus 5cm added to the length and width to allow for turnings. The upper piece may be lining fabric as it will not be seen.

Attach the four valances to the canopy, with the lining side of the valance to the right side of the lower canopy, raw edges level. The gathers should be evenly spaced and the end kept within the seam allowances [3.20]. Press the seam towards the canopy.

Press 2.5cm in all round the top piece of the canopy, forming mitres at the corners. Tack the corners. Pin the two canopy sections together, wrong sides together, so that all the turnings are enclosed. Topstitch all round close to the edge.

Ruched canopy For a ruched canopy, cut the lower rectangle to 1½ times the length of the finished length. Gather down the sides before joining it to the valances.

Corona and drapes

If you have an ordinary bed but want to achieve a luxurious effect, try a corona bedhead with drapery. A substantial amount of fabric is involved so you could consider making the drapery in net, which would be lighter and softer and less expense than if you used a heavier fabric.

Originally, it was usual to make both the bedhead and the bedspread in the same fabric as the corona, giving a rich and luxurious impression. Contrasting fabrics could be just as effective.

The corona consists of a backcloth behind the bedhead and two side curtains joined to it, held back from the bed by being draped over ornamental projections called 'ombres'. Fabric tiebacks attached to ornamental wall hooks or rings are easy to make and would be equally attractive. The curtains and backcloth are hung from an overhead projection – the corona itself – which is trimmed with a pelmet to hide the curtain rail. It used to be the practice to buy a metal corona with

3.21 The critical measurements for a corona and drapes

all the fittings attached. They are still available but you could make one yourself and improvise the necessary fittings.

Planning the corona and drapery is important, so study pictures and examples and make a scale drawing in order to get the proportions right [3.21]. A corona is usually about 240cm from the floor. The ombres or other fixtures should be about 15cm higher than the top of the bed, and situated between 30cm and 40cm out from the sides. Experiment with a sheet to see what will suit your bed best.

The length of the backcloth will be the height of the corona to the floor. Its width will be the width between the draping points. Allow twice the fullness of fabric. The backcloth is generally left unlined.

To measure for the side curtains, drape a tape in a graceful curve from the centre front of the corona, down to where the curtains will be tied back, and then straight to the floor. Add a total of 7.5cm for top turnings and hem. A 120cm width is adequate for each curtain. Remember to buy enough for two curtains. They may be lined with the same fabric, or curtain lining or net.

Also include enough fabric and lining for the corona and its fabric pelmet, and for the tie-backs. The pelmet depth is normally an eighth of the total drop. Measure round the curved edge and make up widths of fabric to double that measurement to allow for fullness.

To make your own corona, prepare a semi-circle of plywood (5-ply is best). The measurement is flexible but for a double bed it would be about 80cm along the straight back edge, and 22cm in depth from the back (the radius). For a single bed version, 50cm along the back extending to 22cm at the front of the curve would be about right.

The underside of the corona must be covered. Use the plywood as a pattern, cutting the fabric a little larger so that you can turn under the raw edges. Screw in six small hook eyes at intervals of 6 or 7cm, just in from the edge of the corona's curve, and a few along the back straight edge. Remove them, glue the turned-in fabric in place, and refit them into the same holes through the fabric.

Make a pelmet as described on page 31, long enough to go round the curve from wall to wall. Pin it to the top of the board, or tack it round the front edge with tacks under the trimming. Fit the board to the wall with a couple of strong brackets.

Make up the side curtains with attached linings except that the tape should be sewn on to the right side of the fabric – otherwise you will be looking up at the working fixtures of the curtain as you lie in bed. The lining or self-lining should be lockstitched to the curtain.

Lightly chalk out the shape of the backcloth on the floor, marking the pelmet width, the width between draping points at the sides of the bed, and the relevant lengths. Now drape the back-cloth fabric on the floor, drawing it up to accommodate the fullness. Trim away the excess fabric equally on both sides. Turn up a double hem at the bottom and sides and fit a curtain tape to the top on the wrong side.

Slip stitch the side curtains to the backcloth fabric. Sew tapes on the wrong side of the side curtains for fixing to the ombres, or make tie-backs (page 40). Hang the backcloth to the hook eyes along the back of the corona, and the side curtains round the curve of the pelmet. Overlap the two front edges. Drape the fabric gracefully over the ombres at the shoulders of the bed, and tie them with the tapes, or fit up the drapery with the tie-backs.

There are a number of variations. You might dispense with the backcloth, hang the side curtains from a pole fixed to the ceiling (through a ceiling joist) at right angles to the wall, give the curtains frilled edges, or trim them and the pelmet with fringing or braid.

DRESSING-TABLE COVER

You may have a kidney-shaped dressing-table which is the traditional style for this cover with its skirt and short valance, but any small chest of drawers, table or even basin unit can be treated similarly in order to bring it into your bedroom or bathroom's decorating scheme.

Most kidney-shaped dressing-tables have a piece of protective glass cut to the shape of the top surface, but if yours is without glass you should be prepared to wash the fabric often. A cotton/polyester mix would therefore be a good choice, or you could make the skirt in an easy-care cotton with the top and valance cut from matching quilted fabric. You will need to pad and/or stiffen the top if you don't use quilted fabric. Hand quilting or patchwork could be worked into the valance, or embroidery or appliqué work. Also consider piping round the top edge.

For the skirt curtains you will need 1½ times the circumference of the top of the piece of furniture, whatever the shape. Divide that figure by the width of the material on the roll to find out how many widths you will need. The depth of the skirt will be from the curtain track to 1cm above the floor, plus a total of 10cm for heading and hem. Multiply that depth by the number of widths needed for the curtains to calculate how much fabric to buy.

The valance will need the same width of fabric to a depth of about 15cm; allow about 5cm on top of that for the seam allowance and the hem.

The top can probably be cut from one width of fabric – measure the dressing-table from front to back and add this on.

A feature of the kidney-shaped dressing-table is its overhanging top which allows room to attach a curtain track. You will have to fix an overhanging top to any furniture that does not allow for curtain track space. If there are no drawers, such as below a basin unit, easy access to the area behind the curtains is less important, so you could dispense with the track and hang the curtains on a plastic-coated wire. Adapt the principle outlined on page 38 – the wire should grip the sides of the unit so that the curtains don't dip. Buy curtain track to fit round the dressing-table, allowing for a centre-front overlap of about 3cm – more will hinder access to the drawers. Fix the track to the underside of the overhang.

Make up and hang the curtains in the usual way. The only opening will be at the centre front.

You could enclose the edges with contrasting binding as an alternative to taking the hems up normally.

To make the top, cut a pattern from brown paper to the exact size of the surface. From the pattern cut out the fabric (and wadding and lining if necessary) allowing an extra 2.5cm all round for seams.

Pin the fabric, wadding and lining together and tack all round the seam line. Sew on piping if you are using it, clip into the seam allowances to enable the piping to curve properly.

Make up the valance, again binding the hem if you like, but don't finish the top edge. Instead, gather it up and pin it round the top piece, clipping into the seam allowance. Neaten the seams by hand overcasting or machine-zigzagging.

4 Loose covers and cushions

Apart from keeping the furniture in good condition, loose covers can be made in various fabrics so that you can change the appearance and character of a room in a few minutes. As the cover becomes dirty, you simply take it off and wash it or have it dry-cleaned.

Instead of trying to protect a new piece of furniture, you may want to cover an old chair or sofa. First make sure that the basic structure is solid and that the existing cover is clean. Vacuum the chair including down the crevices and underneath, and shampoo and mothproof it if necessary. Check the casters before you measure for the fabric because the height of the chair may be affected if you have to change them.

Loose covers are not suitable for covering leather, plastic or wicker chairs; a velvet base is difficult too because the pile prevents the loose cover from lying correctly. The fabric should not be too thick, as at many points in the construction several layers have to be sewn together, especially where piping is involved. Plain fabric tends to show spots, sewing errors and creases. Slubbed and loose-woven materials are not suitable and dressmaking fabrics are unlikely to be hard-wearing enough. Fabric with a large pattern is uneconomical because you have to centre the main motifs, and the apparently bold effect when seen on the roll may be lost on a small chair.

The ideal fabric to choose therefore is one that is hard-wearing, pre-shrunk, fade- and crease-resistant, of good quality and with a pattern which will allow for the most economical cutting and won't show spots or minor mistakes. Linen union, damask, heavy cotton or a repp are popular choices.

You may only ever want to dry-clean your loose covers, but if you do plan to wash them yourself, ask the shop assistant's advice about shrinkage when buying the fabric. If you wash the cover, fit it back on the chair while it is still slightly damp so that if any shrinkage has occurred the cover can stretch back to its proper size. Iron it on the chair.

ARMCHAIR COVER

Tools and materials
Apart from the fabric, you will need a fabric tape measure, tacking cotton, ordinary cotton thread (two or three reels per chair) in the predominant colour of the fabric, medium-weight piping cord (probably grade 2 or 3), a 30–45cm zip or length of Velcro, or hooks and eyes (size 0), sharp cutting-out scissors, steel pins (preferably with glass heads), a piping or zipper foot for the sewing-machine (it is not feasible to consider sewing a loose cover by hand), a packet of suitable sewing-machine needles, dressmaker's chalk, graph paper and an iron. Upholstery skewers would also be a help.

Measuring the chair
An average chair takes 7m of fabric or five times the height of the back of the chair. (You should use this only as a figure for costing the project.) Accurate measurement is essential to establish the actual length of fabric to buy. You may find it helpful to draw a chart of the chair parts, marking in the dimensions [4.1].

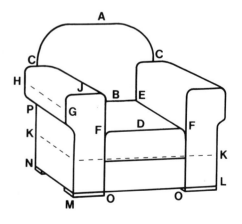

4.1   Measuring points for a cutting list

The main project described here is a relatively simple design for a straightforward armchair. It has piping round the outside back, along the outer arm, and round the arm front. There is also a skirt (or valance) with three variations, all with piping running along the top. Later in the section are instructions for other styles of chairs, and adaptations for a sofa cover are given. Cushion covers are described on page 95.

The cutting list is as follows:

Inside back	(× 1)
Seat	(× 1)
Front border	(× 1)
Inside arm	(× 2)
Outside arm	(× 2)
Front arm panel	(× 2)
Outside back	(× 1)
Skirt	(*optional – see below*)

Write down the list, with any additional parts your chair might have, such as wings or seat cushions, and add the measurements to the cutting list. Use a fabric tape measure to establish the chair's dimensions. The measurements will all be rectangles to facilitate the cutting out – the pieces will be trimmed to the correct shape at the fitting stage.

Inside back Measure from the top rear edge of the chair down to the point where the inside back meets the seat (**A–B**). Add 15cm for a tuckaway. Add a total of 5cm for the two seams at the top and bottom. The tuck-away is a generous allowance of fabric which you push down between the seat and back, and between the seat and arms, when you have sewn the whole cover together. It is designed to give you some latitude in fitting the cover to the chair, and you will find that you can smooth the finished cover into a good fit by pushing and adjusting the tuck-away. It also helps to hold the cover in place without it creasing.

Measure the width of the inside back at its widest point and add 5cm for the seams (2.5cm at each side).

Seat Measure from the point where the seat meets the inside back, to the peak of the middle of the front edge (**B–D**). Add 15cm for the tuck-

away at the back, and a total of 5cm for the seams. Measure across the seat at the widest point to where the seat meets the inside arms (either **E–E** or **F–F**). Add 30cm to give a 15cm tuck-away at each side, and a further 5cm for the side seams (2.5cm at each side).

Inside arm First determine the line along the top outer curve of the arms (**G–H**), where the inside and outside arms will meet. The design of the chair may dictate the position. In most loose covers, this line is defined by a length of piping, and because it is conspicuous it needs to be well balanced. Mark along it with several pins if it is not obvious. Measure the height of the inside arm from the point where it meets the seat, to the line you have marked (**F–G**). Add 15cm for the tuck-away. Add a further 5cm for 2.5cm seams at top and bottom.

Measure the length of the line from where the top of the arm meets the front panel of the arm (**J**), to where the inside and outside back meet near the top of the arm (**C**). This will give you the longest dimension for the inside arm piece. If you measure it at any other point you may cut it too short. Add 5cm for the two 2.5cm seams. Allow for two inside arms.

Outside arm This is the first stage at which you should consider fitting a skirt. The skirt is not essential but it does give a good finish to any chair or sofa which is upholstered to floor level. It is not appropriate for certain kinds of chair, for example a wing chair with curvy carved legs.

First settle the height of the skirt: 12–15cm will probably be about right. To give an ample working margin, measure for the outside arm from a position 8–10cm above the floor, to the pinned line at the top of the outside arm (**K–H**). Add 2.5cm for the seam at the top. If you are not having a skirt, measure right down to the floor.

Measure the width of the outside arm from the edge of the front arm panel to the outside back (**G–H**). Add 2.5cm for each seam at the front and back. Allow for two of these parts.

Front arm panels If there is to be a skirt it will meet the bottom of these panels, so measure the height from the top of the arm (**J**) to your point 8–10cm above the floor (or else down to the floor). Add a generous 5cm for two seams. Measure the width across the panel from the inside arm to the outside arm at the widest point. Cut two of these pieces.

Front border Again, if you are making a skirt it will cover the bottom of this piece, so measure from the front edge of the seat (**D**) down to your line 8–10cm from the floor. Add 2.5cm for that seam. Otherwise, measure down to the floor. Measure the width from the inside arm at one side to the inside arm at the other (**F–F**), and a total of 5cm for the two seams. Allow for just one piece.

Outside back Measure from the top of the back (**A**) to the floor or skirt line (8–10cm from the floor), and across the back at its widest point. Note that many chairs have a bulge where the arms meet the back. Take this into account to avoid being short of material at a later stage. Add 5cm to both height and width for the seams. Cut one piece only.

Skirt For a corner kick-pleat skirt you will need one width of fabric for each side, plus one for the front and one for the back – four widths altogether. Add 5cm to each length for turnings. The depth will be 12–15cm plus 5cm for a double hem at the bottom, plus 2.5cm for the seam at the top (19.5cm–22.5cm). You will also need three rectangles of fabric for the backs of the pleats, each the depth of the side panels and 30cm wide, and two half-pleats for the back opening of the same depth and 20cm wide.

For a frilled or flounced skirt, you will need four pieces, two double the length of **LM** and two double the length of **MN**. A less generous frill can be achieved with pieces 1½ times the length of each side. The joins will occur at the four corners.

For box pleats you will need to join strips of fabric to a length that is three times the total length round the bottom of the chair, plus about 10cm for the side hems. The depth of the strips will be about 20cm. You will probably be able to cut the strips from surplus fabric but remember that the pattern must run vertically on all of them.

A plain hem suitable for big boxy chairs or for wing chairs is achieved by carrying the front, back and side panels down to the base of the chair and then tying them underneath. Allow enough fabric to make four strips, each 10cm by the measurement between the legs.

Arm caps will extend the life of the loose cover since the tops of the arms get more wear than anywhere else. Allow half a metre extra for each arm cap.

Piping Piping gives style and strength to the chair cover. If you plan to make it in a contrasting fabric to the main cover, calculate your cutting requirements separately. Otherwise, add piping to your main list. As a rough guide, a panel the size of the chair seat should provide enough material to cover piping. You may be able to get some of the material out of the leftover pieces from the main cutting scheme. Refer to page 80 for the details of how to cut and sew piping. Remember that it should always be cut on the bias (diagonally to the selvedge) to give flexibility in use.

Estimating the fabric

You now have all the necessary measurements. One of the easiest ways to work out how much fabric to buy is to mark out with chalk an area on the floor the width of the chosen fabric, probably 120cm or 130cm. Cut out rectangular pieces of newspaper to correspond to all the cover's sections (don't forget the cushion if you are planning to make one), label them and lay them within the chalked confines in the most economical way you can find, making sure that all the lengths run parallel to the edges.

4.2a and b [a] Plot the pieces on graph paper. [b]
Transfer to the fabric with adjustments for pattern
matching
a outside back
b outside arm
c inside arm
d inside back
e seat
f front border
g skirt
h front arm

If the fabric has a large pattern with central
motifs, chalk off on the floor the length of the pattern repeat and the approximate position of the
motif, so that you can place the focal points of the
loose cover accordingly. (Remember that the
motif for the centre inside back will be nearer the
top of the rectangle, as the bottom 15cm of the
piece will form the tuck-away.) See [**4.2b**] for a
typical layout plan.

Decide whether there will be enough fabric
left over down the sides for the piping or whether
you will need to add on to the end a panel the size
of the chair seat (as explained above). When you
have found the best arrangement, measure the
total length of the chalked area – this will be the
amount of fabric to buy.

An alternative method for estimating the
required amount of fabric is to make a scale drawing on graph paper, with one small square repre-
senting 10mm, say. Cut a length of graph paper
the scaled-down width of the fabric and cut similarly scaled-down rectangles to represent the
various sections to lay on top of it. Mark the positions of central motifs. Don't forget to label
everything [**4.2a**].

Whichever method you use, keep a record of
the sequence you have arranged the pieces in so
that you can refer to it when cutting out the
fabric. It is best to round up your total measurement to the next full metre.

When you have bought your fabric you should
go through the measuring process again as you
cut each piece. One mis-measurement could ruin
the whole operation, so it is worth spending extra
time at this stage.

Cutting out
For cutting, refer to the sequence you devised
when estimating how much fabric to buy. Lay or
pin each piece in its position on the chair as you
go, or set them to one side, but whichever you do,
be sure to label everything. You will also find it
helpful to mark the top, bottom and straight grain
on each piece.

Cut simple rectangles at this stage – you will be
trimming them to the exact shapes of the parts at
the fitting stage.

73

4.3   Pin the inside back to the chair

Fitting the cover

Now you can start to fit the pieces in place. The first stage is to pin them all together with both the right side of the fabric and the pinned seams facing you. At a later stage you will be turning all the seams into the inside, but if you pin carefully now you won't have to tack all the sections together later.

Lay the inside back in position and secure it with pins or upholstery skewers. On this style of cover, in which the inside back meets the outside back, you may have to form a dart or at least ease the excess fabric by gathering it up at the corners. This will be unnecessary on a chair which has a separate panel or border across the top of the back.

Draw the excess fabric up into a fold at right angles to the edge of the chair back. Push in a line of pins snugly against the upholstery of the chair to mark where the dart will be sewn [4.3]. If there is a lot of surplus fabric it would be better to make several small darts. When you come to pin the outside back to the inside back later on, you will be able to check the size and positioning of the darts.

Next, lay the rectangle cut for the seat in its place. Make sure that it is centrally positioned with a 2.5cm overhang at the front, and push a couple of pins or skewers through it to hold it

temporarily. At the rear of the seat, you will have a 15cm tuck-away to match the tuck-away of the inside back. Smooth out both of these, and pin them together 2.5cm from the edges. If they do not match, trim off the excess from the longer piece. This operation does not have to be too precise because the fabric will be pushed down inside the body of the chair.

Take up the two pieces for the inside arms and lay them in place. If there is a pattern on your fabric, the pieces should, of course, be mirror images of each other. Make sure the pattern is upright and, even if there is no pattern, ensure that the grain of the fabric runs vertically. Push pins or upholstery skewers through the fabric into the chair to hold the material temporarily. At the bottom, there will be a tuck-away. Pin it to the seat tuck-away, just as you pinned the seat and inside back tuck-aways together. At the top, the fabric will follow the line of the chair arm and extend beyond the piping line or the line you marked earlier with pins. If the chair arm tapers, there will be an excess of material at the narrower end, so trim this off a few centimetres outside the piping line to give clearer access to your work. At the front, the fabric should extend 2.5cm beyond the line of the chair arm. Check that it does, and insert a couple of pins to hold it in place.

4.4 Pin the inside arms and seat into place

Now deal with the rear part of the inside arms. This will be the first area that offers any complications. There are already two tuck-away pieces (the inside back and the seat) pinned together to form a seam. There are also to be tuck-aways to the inside arms, both along the side of the seat (**FE**), and up the first few inches of the gap between the chair back and the inside arm (**EC**).

Pin the inside arm tuck-away to the seat tuck-away, starting at the rear of the seat. Pin along a line 2.5cm in from the two edges to give a sewing line. Now draw the three pieces of the fabric together, and start pinning vertically up the seam between the inside arm tuck-away and the inside back tuck-away [**4.4**].

Feel inside the uncovered chair to establish where the recess ends between the back and the arm. From here upwards there will be no tuck-away, and from here downwards the tuck-away

will have to taper outwards to the bottom. Insert a pin so that the two panels of fabric lie snugly against the chair. Working down the seam, make a neat line in pins from that point to the point where the three sections of fabric join at the bottom. Above that point, put in another line of pins to follow the line between the chair back and the chair arm [**4.4**]. You will find that the fabric resists following the line of the curve, so snip into the seam turnings as often as is necessary to ease the tension, but not further in than the line of pins.

Do not expect to get a perfect fit first time at this part of the project. You will probably have to re-pin the work several times until you get a satisfactory fit, with a neat seam close against the upper part of the chair arm merging into an increasing quantity of tuck-away in the recess. Repeat the procedure for the other inside arm.

4.5 Pin the outside arms and front arm panels to the chair

You can now fit the outside arms. If there is a pronounced slope in the design of the arm of the chair, you will have plenty of fabric to spare. Make sure, however, that you fit this piece upright with any large motifs centrally positioned. There should be 2.5cm seam allowances at the front and back of the chair. Position the fabric so that it extends below the line of the skirt or, if there is to be a tie-under, so that it brushes the floor. Pin the fabric in place to meet the piping line at the top (**GH**), and trim off the excess to give a 2.5cm seam allowance.

You can now merge the inside and outside arms into a good join. Check that your piping line (**GH**) is well placed and follows a smooth straight line along the outer top part of the chair arm. Draw the two seam allowances together, and pin them as close to the arm as you comfortably can without straining the fabric. Fit the outside arm on the opposite side.

Now fit the arm front panels [**4.5**]. Push four or five pins or upholstery skewers through each

4.6   Add the seat border

4.7   Push down the tuck-aways to check they fit the recesses

panel to keep it in position. Make sure that any pattern is vertical, and that the two panels are mirror images of each other. Each one should overlap the outer edge of the chair arm by 2.5cm all round, and hang down generously below the line of the skirt.

Pin all round the panels, forming a seam between the arm front and the inside and outside arm pieces. There will eventually be piping round this line, so make sure that the seam falls exactly on the crest of the arm – otherwise the piping will droop down the arm front or drag back along the arm top. You may have to make a few tiny darts round the crest [**4.5**].

Make a neat join at **G** where the arm front meets the seam of the inside and outside arms. Trim off any excess to give a tidy seam all round.

The seat border comes next. Pin it in place with the pattern or the grain of the fabric running vertically. Pin the seam allowance at the top to the seam allowance of the seat itself, exactly on the crown of the curve (**FF**). Pin the seam allow-ance at each side to the seam allowance on the arm fronts (**OF**).

You will find that these three parts – arm front, seat and seat border – all meet at or near **F**. If you push your hand down into the recess along the side of the seat (**FE**), you can establish how far down you can take the corresponding recess in your loose cover. Mark the position on the front arm panel with a pin. Push the tuck-away ends of the inside arm and the seat down into the gap – you pinned them together earlier but now check that the tuck-away is tapered from front to back to fit the recess. Pin round the seam between the seat and the seat border, and along the seam between the inside arm and the front arm panel. When you reach the point you have marked with a pin to show the depth of the gap, start pinning together the seat border and the arm panel, right to the bottom of those pieces of fabric [**4.6 and 4.7**].

Repeat the operation at the other side of the seat border.

4.8   Fit the outside back

For fitting the outside back you may find it helps to tip the chair forward on to its arm fronts. Ensure that the fabric is exactly centred if there is any kind of pattern. To do this, measure to find the centre of the chair back and mark it with pins or chalk at top and bottom. Find the centre of the fabric by folding it, and line it up with the pins or chalk marks. Pin the fabric in place so that there is a 2.5cm seam allowance at the top. It should reach to just below the level of the skirt (or brush the floor if you are having a simple hem).

Pick up the seam allowance of the inside back along the top of the chair, and the seam allowance of the outside back, and pin the two together along the line of the crest of the chair back (**CAC**). This line will have piping, so position it as accurately as possible. Re-adjust any darts pinned in the inside back if necessary.

As you take your line of pins down the side of the chair, you will arrive at the area where three or even four parts of the loose cover meet: inside arm, outside arm, inside back and outside back. They come together at **C** where the chair arm meets the chair back, where there may be a pronounced bulge. Forming neat seams here can be difficult. If the turnings of one seam overlap

those of another, fold them down together to avoid excessive bulging. If the outside back seam is unwilling to round any curves, snip it to ease the tension. Continue pinning down the right side as far as the hem or the top of the skirt.

Fit this part of the work snugly but not too tight or it will strain the fastening at the opposite side of the back should any shrinkage occur later. Loose covers are not meant to be as perfectly fitted as tacked-on upholstery covers so there is some latitude, and a slight fullness is preferable to a pulled, strained appearance.

As far as fastenings are concerned, the choice is between a zip, Velcro, and hooks and eyes. The opening can be at either side, though to have it at the left is more usual.

Mark the point at which the fastening will begin [**4.8**]. As a rough guide the opening will be 30–45cm long. On the type of chair illustrated, the correct point is 6–8cm down from **P**. On a balloon-backed chair the fastening should close to the widest point on the back. Mark the top of the opening with pins or dressmaker's chalk, and draw the seams together. Pin them temporarily.

Go round all the seams again to check that the pinned seams fit as well as possible.

4.9   Mark the line of the skirt

Marking the seams

Mark all the seams for sewing by going right round the chair and trimming all the seam turnings so that they are an exact 2.5cm on both pieces of fabric. Then, at intervals of 8–10cm, cut a notch into the seam turnings through both pieces of fabric at the same time. Make the notches between a half and one centimetre deep, and roughly triangular in shape. Cut them at slightly irregular intervals in slightly different shapes and sizes so that when you are trying to sew a bundle of fabric on which the seams appear to bear no relation to each other, you can line up the corresponding notches.

Now mark the line of the skirt. With a small ruler, go right round the chair and push in pins at exactly the point the skirt will be sewn to, at intervals of 10–12cm. The skirt should eventually clear the floor by about half a centimetre, so add this clearance to your measurement – say 12.5cm for a 12cm skirt. Take care to insert a pin close to each side of every seam so that you will get absolute accuracy at these critical points.

Alternatively, you can mark a line with dress-maker's chalk if the fabric will take it clearly [**4.9**].

The cover is now fully fitted (without the skirt), and providing you sew along the marked lines you will be able to take off the cover for sewing and put it back again with the exact fit repeated.

Remove all the pins which have skewered various parts to the chair, and carefully lift the cover away. You might find it helpful to pin on again the identification labels.

79

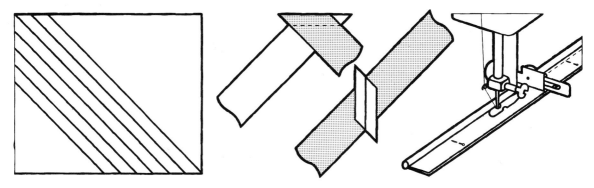

4.10a, b and c   Making up the piping: [a] Cut the casing
on the bias. [b] Join the strips at right angles and press
open to finish. [c] Insert the cord and machine close to it

Making up the piping

Before you sew the cover itself, make up your
supply of piping. Piping is the thin roll which on
many chairs and cushions runs along the seam
lines to define them and help protect weak areas
from wear.

Designers of modern upholstery sometimes
dispense with piping. Others take advantage of
its design potential by making it in a different
fabric from the rest of the cover, so that it gives
extra definition to the shape of the chair or sofa.

Piping is easy to make and consists of lengths
of piping cord covered by and sewn into a long
strip of fabric folded in two. Piping cord is available in thicknesses graded from 1 to 6. A medium
grade, 2 or 3, is suitable for general use. Most
suppliers stock only one grade. If you are
planning to wash the loose cover rather than
dry-clean it, you will need to boil the cord first as
it will shrink quite badly otherwise. Pre-shrunk
piping cord can be bought.

Mark out the fabric for your piping. Cut it into
strips 6cm wide on the bias (diagonally to the selvedge). Fabric cut on the bias has more 'give'
than if cut on the straight grain so is better able to
follow the contours of upholstery seams. Make

your first cut straight across the diagonal of the
square, then further cuts on each side of it
[**4.10a**].

Machine-sew the cut pieces into a continuous
strip. Lay the first two end to end in a V-shape,
with the right sides together. They should overlap by about 1cm. Machine-sew about 1cm in
from the ends. The seam will run between the
two angles formed at the overlapping points
[**4.10b**].

Sew on each section in turn to produce a continuous length. Turn it wrong side up on the
ironing-board and press open the seam at each
join. Snip off the small triangles of excess fabric
along the sides of the strip [**4.10b**].

Take the length back to the sewing-machine,
together with the roll of piping cord. Install the
piping (zipper) foot.

Fold the beginning of the strip of fabric, wrong
sides together, and insert the piping cord. Keeping the cord inside the roll well up against the
piping foot, sew along the whole length [**4.10c**].
You will produce a continuous firm roll of fabric
with the cord inside it, and with two seam turnings about 2.5cm wide. The piping is now ready
to use.

4.11 Insert the piping by pinning or tacking and then machine-stitching

Sewing the cover

In principle, the process of sewing the cover is perfectly simple. In reality, of course, there are complications that can appear fearsome on the first cover you sew. You have to handle a bundle of apparently random fabric, full of pins, all of which seem to be hidden or in the wrong place. Furthermore, you will have to sew piping into some of the seams as you go. You will have to get used to identifying which part you are working on, and to turning some part of the cover inside to outside several times in the course of the operation. The idea is to work gradually round the cover inverting a seam and then sewing the re-pinned seam, including any piping, before going on to the next.

Withdraw a few pins at a time, invert the seam and re-pin it using the same holes as far as you can. As each seam becomes inverted the turnings will lie on the inside of the cover. The notches and edges should be positioned exactly as they were when you fitted the cover.

Take the cover to the sewing-machine, and start to feed the re-pinned seam through it. Sew along the pin line, withdrawing each pin as it arrives at the sewing foot. If you turn and sew all your seams accurately, your cover should be the same size and shape, and therefore the same fit, as it was when you pinned the individual pieces of fabric on the chair.

Start with the darts at the top of the back. Turn them to the inside of the cover and sew them in position (you may feel more confident if you tack them first). Open each dart out on both sides of the sewing line and press it open. Tie the ends of the threads.

Turn next to the seam that joins the inside arm to the inside back (**CE**). This is the seam that forms a tuck-away in its lower half, fitting closely against the chair in its upper part. Continue by sewing the inside back to the seat along the tuck-away seam, and then by sewing the inside arm to the seat. Start at the rear of the seat, where two seams already meet. Form the next seam from that corner. It will follow, if you recall, the sewing line that you adjusted to meet the deepest point of the recess between the chair seat and arm. Sew along that seam, but stop sewing at a point 5cm from the end. You will see the reason shortly.

The cover is now beginning to take shape, with the four main inner panels fitted in place. None of the seams for those panels has needed piping. Almost all the remaining seams on the chair *will* require piping, so re-insert the piping foot in your machine.

The first piped seams to sew are those joining the inside arm to the outside arm. There are several methods. One is to invert the seam as usual, then feed in the piping as you sew, removing the pins as each one arrives at the sewing foot. However, this involves working your piping into a narrow space between two pinned seam turnings.

One alternative – a time-consuming one but which may be the easiest in the long run – is to unpin the seam, insert the piping, and either re-pin or tack it with the piping in place. Then the sewing is easy [**4.11**].

4.12   Joining piping at a T-junction

4.13   Joining piped seams around the outside arm, seat and seat border

4.14   Snip into the seam where the opening will start

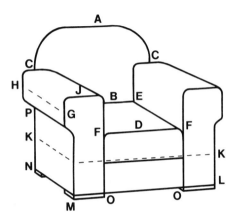

Otherwise, you might like to dispense with re-pinning and sew the seams 'freehand'. You can bring the two seams together as they approach the sewing foot, and feed in the piping, lining up the two edges of the piping and the two edges of the seam turnings as you proceed. Take care to line up the notches – this may not be easy because adding the piping tends to cause the lower layer of fabric to pucker. The upper layer of fabric will then seem longer than the lower one. Do not be deceived into thinking that the notches were wrong. Instead, pull and ease the fabric through the machine, and make the notches match up accurately.

Whenever sewing piping, you will find it an advantage to arrange the work so that the outer part of any curve in the seam is underneath. This is because the outer curve was slightly longer at the fitting stage so that even if it puckers slightly, the notches in the shorter length will still coincide.

In this case, it means putting the outside arm on the bottom, then the piping, then the inside arm on the top. (Likewise, the inside arm goes on the bottom, followed by the piping, followed by the arm front, when you come to that stage.)

Next sew the arm front panels. Start at the bottom of the outside arm (**K**). Sew the arm front to the outside arm, with piping in the seam.

At the top of the outside arm will be a junction of two piped seams (**G**). Deal with the bulk by cutting a length of the piping cord (but not the casing) at the point where they join. If you consider the junction as a 'T', the upright of the 'T' is the one to cut – in other words, the piping running from **G–H**. Peel back the cover of the piping as far as the sewing line of the seam which crosses the upright, cut the cord, and fold the seam down again [**4.12**].

Alternatively, if your machine is strong enough, sew one piece of piping across the other piece. You can help by lifting the sewing foot and 'walking' your machine across the bulky thicknesses of fabric, turning the wheel manually.

It is best to sew the seam turnings so that they all lie in one direction, pointing towards the floor. Then they are less visible through the finished cover than those which point upwards.

From the fitting stage you will recall dealing with the gap where each side of the seat meets the arm at the front at **F**. You marked its depth with pins or dressmaker's chalk. Also, you left a 5cm pinned seam in the tuck-away between the inside arm and seat where it neared this point.

Now you will have to join together these various items – the seat and front border, the inside arm and arm front, and the remainder of that seam between the seat and inside arm. The front border and arm front must also be joined below the gap. And there will be two sets of piping, one across the front border and one down the arm front, which must merge together.

Sew the piped seam between the arm front and the inside arm down as far as the pin at **F**. Leave enough piping dangling to reach the bottom of the seam eventually. Next sew the piped seam between the seat and seat border (**F–F**). Cut off the cord (not the casing) and roll the remaining piped seam running from **J–O** over the fabric of the piping you have just cut, and continue to sew to the bottom of the new seam. Finally close the 5cm gap betwen the inside arm and the seat [**4.13**].

Again, you may find that with so many thicknesses of fabric at the point where the two piped seams join, an ordinary household sewing-machine cannot cope. If that is the case, raise the sewing foot and 'walk' the work through manually, or finish the seam by hand.

The most difficult part of the job is now over, and you can go on to sew the outside back to the rest of the cover. Locate the point where the zip opening starts, and with the notches accurately arranged, snip into the seams at that point. Invert the seams from there all round the chair back to the bottom on the opposite side. This seam will be piped. Sew from the skirt line (or the hem if you are not having a skirt) on the back only, with the piping in place, joining in the outer arm just below **P** at the top of the opening. Match the notches accurately throughout [**4.14**].

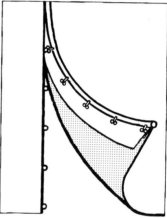

4.15a and b [a] Pin and sew the placket to the opening. [b] Fold round, hem and attach hooks and eyes

The opening
The hooks and eyes method You will have to reinforce the two sides of the opening because the hooks and eyes have to bear the strain of keeping the cover closed against any shrinkage in the material. Measure the length of the opening. Add 2.5cm and cut two pieces of fabric to this length, 7.5cm wide and on the bias of the fabric.

Pin the placket material on top of the piping along the outside back edge of the opening. Sew round the placket [**4.15a**] and take it over the top where the outside back joins the outside arm. Open out the placket and you should see the piping neatly enclosed. Fold the placket round over the raw edges to the wrong side and hem stitch it in place. You can now sew hooks-and-eyes tape to the placket at intervals of 4 or 5cm [**4.15b**].

4.16a, b and c   The stages for attaching Velcro strips to the opening

Velcro Buy enough for the length of opening and the same amount and width of cotton tape or seam binding. Sew one half of the Velcro and the tape together, wrong sides facing each other, down one side. Insert the raw edge of the outside back into them and tack it in place. Pin and then sew the opposite length of Velcro to the outside arm opening, overlapping it by about 15mm. Bring the Velcro strips together at the top of the placket, pin them and then machine across the top. Fold the second Velcro strip to the outside so that the raw edge is enclosed and hem it in place [**4.16a, b and c**].

Zip You will need to use the zipper or piping foot on the machine. Turn under the raw, unpiped edge and tack it in place [**4.17a**]. Lay the closed zip under this edge, right side up and with the opening end of the zip at the bottom. Pin and tack it. Bring the piped edge over the zip and tack along the edge of the piping [**4.17b and c**]. From the right side, and starting at the top, stitch down close to the cord. Open the zip. Stitch across the top of the opening and down the other side [**4.17d**]. It is important to sew the two sides of the zip in the same direction so that the material won't pull. Trim the turnings evenly with the zip's tape and overcast the edges together.

4.17a, b, c and d   The stages for putting a zip into the opening

Tie-under finish

For a plain hem that will give an uncluttered, tailored look, especially suitable on chairs such as wing chairs where the legs will show, you will have allowed in your cutting plan for four strips 10cm deep, by the measurement between each leg, plus 5cm for hems [**4.18**].

Finish the cover itself and apply the fastening. Cut the sides of the four strips to a slight angle and hem them. The bottom hem should be slightly wider to form a casing. Pin and then stitch the casings to the base of the cover between the legs [**4.19**].

Cut a 5cm wide facing to fit the shape of each corner and machine it on, right sides together, about 1cm from the edge. Turn the facing and press. Turn under a narrow hem and oversew the edge to the cover [**4.20**].

Introduce a length of tape into the four casings, each long enough to tie comfortably at the ends [**4.21**]. Four more tapes could usefully be sewn on halfway along each casing for tying centrally under the chair – this might help particularly on a large chair or sofa.

4.19   Stitch the strips to the base of the cover

4.20   Make facings to neaten the corners

4.18   The edges improved by a tie-under finish

4.21   The tie-unders fitted with tapes and tied into place

85

4.22   Sew piping to the cover before attaching the skirt

4.23   Pin the skirt to the cover, cutting notches all round

Making the skirt

If you are planning to have a skirt, you will have already determined its design in the planning stages. Its correct height off the floor should be marked with a line of pins or dressmaker's chalk on the sewn cover. Regardless of the style of skirt, it is easiest to sew on the piping at this stage. Sew it on to the cover, starting and finishing at the opening, so that the corded part is uppermost and the raw edges point to the floor. Make one end abut with the piping running down the back half of the opening by peeling back the casing and cutting the cord level, then tucking the end of the casing down into the seam [**4.22**].

Corner pleats The simplest and most economical design of skirt, suitable for a wide range of chairs, has straight sides and inverted kick-pleats at the corners. You will already have cut four panels, two the length of the sides, and one each the length of the back and the front of the chair, plus seam turnings. Each piece should have an extra 5cm at the bottom for a double hem, and 2.5cm at the top for the turning. You will also have cut five pieces for the pleats.

Join all the pieces together in this order, using a flat seam, right sides together: half-pleat, left side panel, pleat, front, pleat, right side panel, pleat, back, half-pleat. Mark the vertical centre of each full pleat with dressmaker's chalk or iron in a crease. Press the seams open. Machine-sew a double 2.5cm hem all round the bottom, and give the vertical ends of the half-pleats double 2.5cm hems too.

Pin the strip to the rest of the cover, bringing the centres of the pleats and the ends of the skirt panels to the corners. Trim round to make a neat 2.5cm seam allowance and cut notches at irregular intervals [**4.23**].

Now gradually unpin the skirt and re-pin it so that the seams end up on the wrong side, matching corners, edges and notches. Sew round the seam close to the piping, starting from the back left opening. Neaten the edges. Sew poppers to the edges of the half-pleats so that these form a full pleat.

4.24 Armchair with a frilled or flounced skirt

4.25 Armchair with a box-pleated skirt

4.26 Box pleats prepared in a strip

Frilled or flounced skirt Join in the correct order the four strips of material: left side, front, right side, back. Machine-sew a double 2.5cm hem, and give the vertical ends narrow double hems. Gather up each side individually with two rows of gathering threads. Then pull up each panel to fit the corresponding side of the chair and adjust the gathers, pinning as you go. Trim the seam allowance.

Invert the seam allowance as usual. This time you will have no notches to match up but the depth of the turning will be uniform. Again, re-adjust the gathers, tack and then sew them in position. Neaten the edges [**4.24**].

Box pleats The size of each pleat will be dictated by the length of each side of the chair, but should be approximately 10cm wide. Join the cut-out strips, right sides together, and press the seams open. Take up and machine-sew a double 2.5cm hem along the bottom edge. Starting along the left side of the chair, divide the length into equal pleats leaving about 3cm clear at the beginning – this will form a placket or turning at the opening. Make a cardboard template to form accurate pleats. It should be the exact width and depth of pleat you want. The depth will be from the skirt

line down to 5mm above the floor.

Lay the strip of material out flat, wrong side up. Using the template, mark with chalk or pins the positions of the designated number of pleats for the left side.

Then consider the front of the chair. You may have to cut another template which will yield equal pleats ending at the corners, but it must not differ too much from the first template or the finished effect will look uneven.

The right side will be the same as the left, but you may have to make a third template for the back if the chair is wider at front or back. Form the pleats by bringing the pins or chalked lines together, so that all the seams joining the strips are hidden at the back. At the end of the back there should be more than enough fabric to turn in 3cm to form the other side of the placket. Tack along the top of the pleats [**4.26**].

Bring up the strip of box pleats to the chair cover. The pleats should lie neatly at the corners. Trim the seam allowance and cut notches at irregular intervals. Re-pin the skirt with the seam turnings to the inside, matching corners and notches. Sew round the seam next to the piping. Neaten the edges [**4.25**].

4.27   Positioning the armcaps

4.28   Making a brown paper template

Arm caps

It is worth making a pair of arm caps for the loose cover since the front end of the arm suffers the worst of the wear and gets easily soiled [**4.27**].

Most consist of a front panel ending just below the line of the scroll, or 15–20cm down the arm front if there is no scroll. The front panel is attached to the cap which runs from the outside lower corner of the front panel on the outside arm (**A**), over the arm itself, and down to the point where the seat meets the inside arm of the chair. If there is a cushion, the arm cap should fit neatly between it and the chair arm, where it will be held in place (**B**). If there is no cushion, it can be made to fit a few centimetres into the recess. The arm cap is piped.

Start by making a template or pattern of the front of one of the arms. Bear in mind that you will be making two arm caps, mirror images of each other. Pin a piece of stiff paper (brown paper is ideal) to the front of the arm. Mark round it the shape of the arm by rubbing it with a pencil or the back of your scissors, or by cutting into it to meet the chair, and cutting round the template between the cuts [**4.28**]. Mark on the template the point (**C**) where the arm piping, which runs along the arm back-to-front on the arm covers, meets the arm front panel.

For the other section, take three measurements. The first is from the front of the arm (**D**) to the point where you want the arm cap to end along the top of the arm (**E**). The next is from the bottom lower corner of the outside panel (**A**), up along the line of the scroll as far as **C**, which is

4.29   Piping the armcap

where the inside arm meets the outside arm on the chair itself. The final measurement is from that junction (C), up over the top of the arm and down to B between the cushion and the inside arm. Add 2.5cm to every dimension where there will be a seam and 5cm to every dimension which will end in a hem.

If you have a patterned fabric, you will have to cut the panels that meet at **CL** in such a way that when sewn the pattern on each side of the arm will be the right way up.

To cut the front panel, pin the template to your fabric (right side up). Don't forget the seam and hem allowances – these measurements are most easily marked with dressmaker's chalk.

Pin the sections together, right sides facing outwards, in the same way that you pinned the chair cover. Start by pinning together the two panels over the arm. Sew them together, adding in a length of piping. Open out the piping case at **C** and cut the end of the cord flush with the seam (don't cut the casing itself). Sew round a double 2.5cm hem from **F** to **G**, cutting off excess piping so that the hem will lie flat.

Pin on a second length of piping to run eventually from **A** to **H**, but only sew it on between **J** and **K** for the moment – in other words round from hem to hem. Leave the two ends hanging [**4.29**].

Pin and hand-sew a double 2.5cm hem at the bottom of the front panel (**HA**). Pin that panel to the top section with a 2.5cm seam allowance on both pieces, right sides out, so that the piping running from **C** to **L** matches up with the marked spot on the front panel. Clip round the curves in as far as the seam line to ease the tension.

Re-pin the pieces so that the seam allowance is on the wrong side, matching up the notches. Sew round the top of the arm cap from **K** to **J**, preferably twice for strength.

You will be left with the two ends of piping. Hand-sew together the hems of the front and side at **KH** and **JA**, enclosing the end of the piping into the fold of one hem for a neat finish. Hem the rest of the front panel betweeen **H** and **B** which will tuck down past the cushion or into the chair's crevice.

Make the other arm cap, cutting and sewing every part to make mirror image of the first one. You may want to sew on a couple of strips of Velcro near to point **E** to hold the arm caps in place.

4.30   Loose cover for a wing chair

Wing chair cover
Follow the usual principles, measure at the widest points. Treat the wings as elements separate from the arms, so that you will have four rectangles for each side: inside wing, outside wing, inside arm, outside arm. The horizontal seam at the base of the wing will be a continuation of the top of the arm. The edges of the wings will be piped. Wing chairs rarely have a skirt unless their legs are very ugly, so plan for a tie-under finish.

When you come to fit the cover, deal with the inside and outside back pieces first. Then apply the wing pieces and cut them roughly to the finished shape. You may find it easier to make a paper pattern at this point. Pin the back wings to the outside back and the inside wings to the inside back, making sure that the seams rest snugly against the chair's contours. Pull the outer edges of the wings together. You will have to make a few tiny darts at the tips of the wings. Fit the rest of the chair as usual.

When you come to sew the cover, it is best to tack the wing seams after re-pinning them to the correct side in order to make sure that the darts stay in position [**4.30**].

Cover for a chair without arms

This too will usually have a plain hem with a tie-under finish, though a skirt would be perfectly feasible. The planning, cutting, fitting and sewing stages are as for a conventional armchair. Be especially careful to get a good fit round the tuck-away areas [**4.31**].

Cover for a straight-sided chair

Again, all the same construction principles apply but you will need to make borders to go round the tops of the arms and back. The edges of the borders will be piped [**4.32**].

Sofa cover

Making a cover for a sofa or chesterfield is not much more difficult than for an armchair. As with a chair, check first that the sofa is structurally sound, shampoo and mothproof it if necessary, and replace any broken castors.

Follow the cardinal rules, such as measuring the sofa at its widest, longest and bulkiest points, cutting everything (except the piping casings) on the straight grain, and adding 2.5cm to each seam and 5cm to each hem edge [**4.33**].

When working out a cutting plan, bear in mind that you will need to join widths of fabric to extend over the outside back, inside back, seat and front border. You can use for guidance any existing seams on the sofa; alternatively, if there are cushions, the seams should be lined up with the cushion edges. If you are using a fabric with a considerable pattern, you won't be able to match the pattern *and* follow these seam lines, so the solution is to pipe the seams. If there are no cushions, use a complete fabric width for the centre panels and join other smaller pieces to the sides to make up the required width, trying to achieve a continuity of pattern down the inside back, across the seat and down the front border. On a small two-seater sofa, it is best to have one central seam dividing the two sides.

If you want to give the sofa a straight-sided skirt with kick-pleats, you may want to have two extra pleats along the front and back lined up with the cushion edges or seams.

Remember to allow enough fabric for the piping, especially if you feel you won't be able to make up enough from the offcuts.

Be prepared to adjust and re-adjust the cover

4.31   A chair without arms

4.32   A straight-sided chair

4.33   A sofa cover

at the pinning stage in order to get the best fit. It is worth spending a lot of time measuring and pinning so that when you do eventually sew the seams, they are correct. You may find that tipping the sofa on its front helps, especially when fitting the outside back to the rest of the cover.

Sew with a double row of stitching those seams that will take a lot of wear, such as round the front of the arms, across the top of the back, along the front of the seat. Neaten all the seams by hand.

Instructions for making a skirt or plain hem with tie-unders and for the various types of opening are the same as for a chair loose cover.

CUSHIONS

In most decorating schemes you can hardly have too many cushions. They are an excellent way of using up remnants, particularly expensive fabrics such as tapestry and silk. There are great savings to be had if you make your own cushions since bought ones are expensive. Moreover, this is probably the area in soft furnishing where imagination and creativity can be best tapped. The possible shapes, styles and decorative effects are pretty well infinite. Cushions can be square, round, oval, heart-shaped, cylindrical; they can range in size from tiny scatter cushions to huge floor cushions; they can serve a specific purpose such as lining a window seat, forming a headrest at the back of a bed, or making a kitchen chair more comfortable; they can be utterly plain, or frilled, hand- or machine-embroidered, piped, overlaid with lace, include patchwork, quilting or appliqué work in their construction, have sequinned segments or buttoned, pleated or smocked areas – the range is virtually limitless.

The fabric you choose will obviously be important since smocking, for instance, would only be appropriate on a light fabric that wouldn't get much wear and tear, whereas the fabric for a cushion intended as a headrest would need to be hard-wearing. It is best to have washable fabrics, though cushions involving more complex construction techniques and expensive fabrics will need dry-cleaning.

Making the pad

Whichever style of cushion you are making, it is always best to make the inner pad as a separate element – otherwise you will never be able to clean the cover.

Any upholstery supplier should be able to provide you with a cushion interior or pad of an appropriate size and filling, but you may want to make a pad to your particular requirements. The pad should be 1.25cm *wider* in both directions than the cushion cover so that the finished object will look properly plump. This applies when the filling is feathers, down, kapok or synthetic wadding. If the filling is in the form of plastic foam in block or chip form, the pad should be the same size as the cushion cover.

Down As with duvet fillings, down is the best but

most expensive choice. The casing should be made from downproof cambric and you should wax the stitching lines to prevent the quills poking through the holes. You will need about ½kg to stuff an average-sized cushion.

Feathers You will need about 1kg to fill an average-sized cushion, and the casing should be made from featherproof ticking. The outer cover should not be too thin or the black stripes of the ticking will show through. Waxing the seams would be a good idea here too.

Synthetic fibres These are cheaper fillings and not so luxurious, and they don't plump up so well. However, they are washable, which may be an advantage, and the pad's cover can be made from cheap calico, old sheeting or curtain lining. You will need ½kg for an average-sized cushion.

Kapok This tends to go lumpy and lose its shape, but would be all right for a purely decorative cushion rather than on a utilitarian one – you will need about ½kg for a small cushion.

Plastic foam Whether in a block or chip form, this crumbles and rots if exposed to the sun, even protected by an outer cover. But it is inexpensive. Blocks of foam are particularly useful for welted cushions and can be cut to the correct shape and size with a Stanley knife. For a small bean bag you will need about five cubic feet of polystyrene beads for the filling.

To make the pad, cut out two pieces of casing fabric to the correct size, allowing 1.5cm for turnings. Sew the pieces together with French seams, wrong sides together first, leaving an opening about 15–20cm long for inserting the stuffing. A French seam will reduce the likelihood of the pad bursting.

Turn the seam to the inside and fill the pad. This is best done in the garden or in the bathroom with the door shut, especially when feathers or polystyrene beads are involved. When the cushion is well filled, oversew the gap – being particularly careful to secure the ends of the thread.

Cushion cover

Instructions follow for square, round, heart-shaped and cylindrical (bolster) covers, and for welted or boxed and squab cushions. Any decorative feature should be incorporated in the design before the cushion is made up.

4.34 Piping a cushion

Before you cut out the fabric, it is best to make a paper pattern in order to get the dimensions accurate; and if you use tracing or other semi-translucent paper (e.g. greaseproof) you will find it easier to centre any motifs in the fabric.

Square cushion

For a square cushion, measure the pad over the top from seam to seam. Don't measure the seams themselves. Cut two pieces of fabric with a 1.5cm seam allowance all round. Remember that unless you are using a foam filling the finished cover should be very slightly smaller than the inner pad.

Most cushions benefit in looks and strength by having piped edges (unless they are to have a frill or lace edging). Make up enough piping to go right round the cushion, plus about 3cm. Remember that if you plan to wash the cover, boil the cord first to prevent it shrinking later. The piping covering could be in a contrasting colour.

Piping on a square cushion will lie better if the corners are rounded. Use a saucer to draw round at each corner.

Make up the cushion by dealing with the piping first. Apply it round the seam line of one of the fabric pieces, starting a few centimetres in from a corner. Never start exactly at a corner or in the middle of a side: it will be either too weak or too conspicuous. Pin and machine-stitch it in place, joining the ends by cutting the cord (*not* the casing) of one end so that it abuts with the other. Sew the ends together and tuck them into the seam allowance [**4.34**].

If you don't want to insert fastenings, join the two halves of the cushion together round three sides and a short way along each end of the bottom edge. Neaten the raw edges and turn the cover right side out, insert the pad and slip stitch the opening together. When you come to clean the cover, unpick the hand-stitching to remove the pad.

Otherwise set in the fastening along the bottom edge of the cushion before dealing with the other seams. It should measure 5cm less than the edge. Start by joining only the two bottom edges together by stitching for 5cm at each end, enclosing the piping neatly.

For a zip, turn under the raw, unpiped edge and tack it in place. Lay the closed zip under this edge, right side up. The centre of the teeth should be level with the tacked edge. Pin and tack the zip in place. Bring the piped edge over the zip and tack along the edge of the piping. You could do the final sewing with the zipper (or piping) foot but you may find it easier to hand-sew.

A strip of Velcro is a satisfactory alternative. Line up the outer edge with the piping stitching line. A further possibility is to use 'poppered' tape (the same as that used for duvet covers) or tape with hooks and eyes already sewn on. Attach the tape to the right side of the seam allowance of the opening, making sure that the two sides of the tape correspond. Open the zip, Velcro or tape and sew twice round the other three sides of the cushion which will take a great deal of wear. Clip the rounded corners and press and neaten the seams.

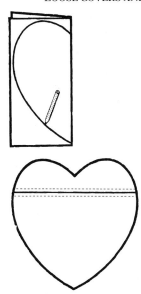

4.35a, b, c and d Round cushion: [a] Draw the template. [b] Divide the back panel. [c] Insert the zip. [d] The zip viewed from the right side

4.36a and b Heart-shaped cushion: [a] Draw the template. [b] Insert the zip at the widest point

Round cushion

Round cushions must be cut very accurately. For both the inner pad and the cover itself you will need to make a paper pattern (again, tracing paper will help to position motifs when you come to cut out the fabric). Decide on the diameter of the cushion and add 3cm for seam allowances. Take the paper (it should be slightly larger than the finished cover) and fold it into quarters. Tie a piece of string round a pencil and attach the string at the centre of the fold with a drawing-pin so that the length of the string is the radius (half the measurement you took first). Draw an arc. Cut round the pencil mark. When you open the paper you should have a perfect circle [**4.35a**].

Once more, you have a choice of openings. The simplest is to leave a gap round a quarter of the circle for slip stitching when the cushion pad has been inserted. If you want to use a zip, Velcro or poppered tape, it is usual to apply it a third of the way down the back of the cover as it is not easy to insert a zip on a curve. The only disadvantage is that the cushion will not be reversible.

Using the paper pattern, cut out the back section of the cushion. Then draw a line across the pattern a third of the way down. Cut the circle into two and arrange the two sectors on the fabric so that they are separated by a 2.5cm gap [**4.35b**].

The gap is where the zip will be inserted. Cut round the sectors giving each the same 1.25cm allowance along the gap. Right sides together, stitch across for 2cm at each end of the join. Insert a zip centrally over the seam, right side upwards, tacking and then machining it [**4.35c and d**].

If using piping, make enough to fit round the circumference and sew it to the other (front) section, first snipping into the seam allowance so that it will lie flat.

Open the zip and pin the front and back of the cover right sides together. Stitch round the seam line right up next to the piping. Clip the curves, turn and press the cover. The pad should slot comfortably through the opening.

Heart-shaped cushion

For a heart-shaped cushion, the same instructions apply for inserting a zip – it should, in this case, run the full width of the cushion [**4.36b**]. In order to make a template you will have to experiment until finding the correct shape and size, fold in half a piece of paper that is slightly larger than you want the cushion to be, and draw a half-heart so that when opened out the two sides will be symmetrical [**4.36a**]. Otherwise, the construction is the same as for a round cushion.

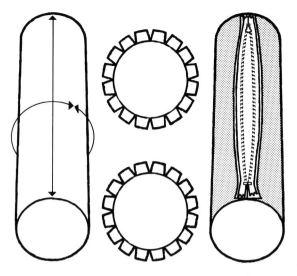

4.37a, b and c   Bolster with plain ends: [a] Measure the bolster girth and length. [b] Apply piping to the end pieces. [c] Insert the zip by hand before sewing on end pieces

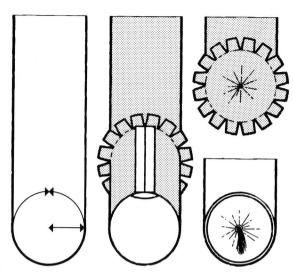

4.38a, b, c and d   Bolster with gathered ends: [a] Measure the end circumference. [b] Sew the end strip in place. [c] Gather the end strip. [d] Sew on a button or tassel at the centre point

Bolster

Traditionally used as head supports on sofas and couches, bolsters are generally firmer than ordinary cushions so pack the filling tightly.

You will need to cut three main pieces of fabric whether you are making the inner pad or the cover. The largest piece will be the length of the finished bolster (plus 2.5cm for seams) by the circumference required. The end circles will have the same diameter [4.37a]. Make a paper pattern for the ends in the manner described for round cushions. If you are using piping apply it to the ends before they are joined to the main section. Clip round the curves before sewing [4.37b].

The zip or other means of fastening should be inserted first [4.37c]. The opening must be quite long – certainly more than half the bolster's circumference. Position the zip centrally and hand-sew into place.

Open the fastening and sew the circular ends to the bolster, clipping into the seam allowances all round. Open the cover right side out and insert the pad.

If you would prefer to have a bolster with gathered ends, cut a strip of fabric for each end to match the circumference of the bolster and as wide as the radius, both plus 2.5cm for turnings [4.38a, b and c]. Join the short sides of the strip and tack one of the long edges to the end of the tube, adding in any piping. Sew round the seam twice for strength. Run a row of gathers (in the same colour as the fabric) along the other long end and draw up tightly. Fasten the thread securely.

Snip round the curves as usual before turning the cover right side out, and sew a tassel or button over the centre [4.38d].

Welted or box cushions

Welted cushions can be square, rectangular, round or shaped to fit an armchair. If making one from scratch, the best filling to use is plastic foam in block form which can be shaped with a sharp blade.

If covering the existing cushions on a chair or sofa, vacuum or shampoo the old cushions when preparing the rest of the chair.

Measure the width, length and depth of the cushion to be covered [**4.39a**]. Cut a top and a bottom piece, and give them slightly rounded corners so that the piping will lie easily. Ensure that any pattern matches up with the chair's inside back panel and the front border.

You will also need to cut fabric for the welt. On a square or rectangular cushion the zip goes at the centre back, and carries round by about 5cm to each side. So for the zip welt cut two strips of fabric, each the length of the back plus 5cm, plus 2.5cm for turnings; their width should be half the depth of the cushion plus 2.5cm for turnings [**4.39b and c**].

The three remaining welt sections are cut so that any pattern runs vertically. The front one will be the width of the cushion plus turnings. The other two will run from the front corners to the start of the zip welt [**4.39d**].

The construction order is: zip inserted into its two half-welts; all the welts joined together in the correct order; piping sewn to both top and bottom sections; welt section stitched to bottom of cover; top cover added to the rest [**4.39e**].

Clip into the curves and snip off the corners as you go, and press the seams.

The only difference when making a round welted cushion is that the zip goes round half the diameter. Its part of the welt is formed in two sections as in [**4.39c**].

For any other shape, for instance a back cushion with indents for the chair arms, it is best to insert the zip across the widest part of the back, adapting the principle outlined for round cushions on page 93.

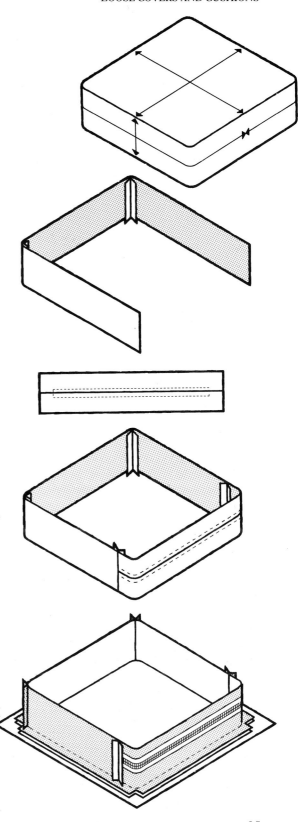

4.39a, b, c, d and e Box cushion: [a] Measure the cushion. [b] Join the welts. [c] Fit the zip halfway down the back welt. [d] Position of the back welt. [e] Insert any piping before attaching the welts to the flat panels

4.40a and b Squab cushion: [a] Attach the ribbons to the cushion corners. [b] Tie the ribbons to the tops of the chair legs

Squab cushion

Squab cushions fit simple wooden chairs and are tied on with ribbons [**4.40b**]. The padding can be as thin or plump as you prefer. For a single cushion you will need 2.4m of ribbon to match or contrast with your fabric.

Lay a sheet of tracing paper over the seat of the chair and draw round its shape. At the same time, mark where the ribbons are to go so that they can tie in pairs round each leg. Cut out a top and bottom piece for the cover, transfer the ribbon positions, and lay the pieces right sides together. Cut the ribbon into 30cm lengths, and pin one at each mark, one end level with the edges of the fabric [**4.40a**]. Sew round the seam, leaving a gap at the back edge through which the cushion pad can be inserted. Turn the cover right sides out, press it, insert the pad and slip stitch the gap closed.

If you want to remove the cover for laundering, insert a zip across the middle of the bottom half, adapting the principle given for a round cushion on page 93.

Decorative techniques for cushions

Patchwork and quilting (pages 14–18) lend themselves particularly well to cushion design. Even a small amount of work can be shown off to great effect.

Another decorative finish would be achieved by making the front of a round cushion in the same style as the buttoned end of the bolster cover on page 94, with a gathered centre.

You could consider giving a cushion a frilled edging like that described for a pillowcase on page 50, or you could simply insert ruched lace edging between the top and bottom cover pieces before sewing them together.

There is one technique particularly applicable to cushion-making – the insertion of a panel framed by the rest of the cover [**4.41a and b**]. The panel can consist of smocking, patchwork, bead or appliqué work, embroidery – whatever you like. You could make it in a 'reverse' fabric of the rest of the cover, such as green flowers on a white background set into white flowers on a green background. Another idea would be to have a large chintz bird or flower set into a plain background, perhaps with an additional border framing it. If you have a lace panel, back the lace with another fabric before you set it in the cushion.

Choose the size of the panel and allow 1.5cm all round for seam allowances. Also decide on the finished size of the cushion and cut two pieces for the cover to those measurements plus 1.5cm all round. If either or both the panel and the cover are to be round, see page 93 for how to cut circles.

Lay the panel either straight or diagonally on top of what will be the top section of the cover and draw round it with dressmaker's chalk. Draw another box or shape of the panel 3cm inside those chalked lines [**4.41a**].

Cut out the material from within this second chalk line. Draw in a third line halfway between the first two. Cut diagonally into the corners as far as this third line and press the seam allowance under by 1.5cm.

Pin the panel under the 'frame' and slip stitch it in place [**4.41b**]. You may have to strengthen the corners with extra stitching where you cut into the seam allowance. If the panel is not hand-worked, you could attach it by machine top-stitching or zigzagging.

STOOL

4.41a and b Panel cushion: [a] Cut out the panel area. [b] Insert the panel

Stools and boxes of any shape can be given loose covers to protect them and to link them with the rest of the decorating scheme. A round stool for a bedroom may look best with a gathered skirt extending from the base of the seat, whereas a lower stool with a larger seat area or a footstool may call for tailored box pleats or inverted corner pleats.

Choose fabric which is hard-wearing enough to be sat on constantly and yet which hangs well. As with larger loose covers, sensible choices would be linen union, damask, heavy cotton or repp. You may have enough left over after re-covering your chair or sofa and will probably want to pipe the main edges.

Before you cover the stool, check to see that its structure is sound. If the seat has sunk a bit you could incorporate a layer of synthetic wadding in the loose cover to build it up.

Cut out pieces of fabric to correspond to the areas to be covered: seat, side borders, skirt, and bias strips for piping. Fabric for the sides and skirt should be cut so that the pattern runs vertically, and the seat should have any major motif positioned centrally.

Fit and make up the cover starting with the seat, padding and lining it if necessary. Then sew the piping to it before you tackle the sides. Sew on the skirt last – see pages 86 and 87 for how to make the different types of skirt. Neaten the seams with hand overcasting.

Pouffe

You may want only to make a new cover for an existing pouffe. To make a new pouffe itself, you will need a hard-wearing fabric such as repp, heavy chintz or even suede – a metre of 120cm fabric will probably be enough; the same amount of calico for lining; strong canvas for the base; a sheet of stiff cardboard; flock, wood shavings or other firm filling; and piping cord. You may find a curved upholstery needle a help, particularly on suede. Plan any decorative features such as quilting (page 14) or appliqué work before you cut and sew the pieces.

For a round pouffe cut the top to your required size plus 1.25cm for seam allowances. See page 93 for making a circular template. The sides are constructed in two panels. Each panel should be the depth of the finished pouffe plus 10cm, and the width of half the circumference of the top plus 2.5cm for seam allowances. There should be ample material left over to cut bias strips for piping.

Cut two sides and *two* tops from the calico, and one top from the cardboard [4.42a]. The canvas circle base should be slightly smaller than these – lose 2cm from the diameter.

Make enough piping to go round the top edge. Pin or tack the piping to the circle of main fabric and stitch round, clipping into the seam allowances to allow the layers to lie properly. Join the side seams of the panels, then join the panels to the top, clipping into their allowances too.

Make up the lining likewise (minus the piping). Turn both the cover and the lining right sides out and fit the lining inside the cover. It will help to anchor the two pieces with invisible stitching where the side seams meet the circles [4.42b].

Fill the pouffe, making sure that there is sufficient stuffing round the top seam. Pack the filling very firmly – if there is not enough the pouffe will soon sag. When the filling is 7cm from the open edges, insert the cardboard and pull the lining panels over it by drawing across double threads [4.42c]. Turn under 1.25cm round the remaining calico circle by pressing or tacking – snip into the seam allowance. Stitch it to the drawn-up lining panels – you may find the curved needle a help here [4.42d].

Draw up the outer panels similarly [4.42e]. Turn under the seam allowance of the canvas base, again snipping into it, and stitch it centrally with double thread [4.42f]. The pouffe is now finished.

A square or oblong pouffe can be made similarly. Gently round the corners by drawing round a saucer so that the piping will lie properly. Insert piping down the four corner seams as well if you want.

For a separate loose cover, cut fabric to match the top and side panels, taking seam turnings into account, and allowing about 5cm for a double 1.5cm hem and 2cm to go under the pouffe. Make up the cover as if you were making the pouffe itself; then turn up the double hem. Sew six tapes at equal intervals round the bottom of the hem so that they can tie centrally under the pouffe [4.42g]. Alternatively, you can insert a length of elastic into the double hem and gather it up so that the cover fits snugly.

4.42a, b, c, d, e, f and g   Pouffe: [a] Main pieces to be cut out. [b] Make up panels and join them to the piped top, then insert the lining. [c] Fill the pouffe, insert the cardboard and draw up the lining. [d] Finish the lining. [e] Draw up the outer panels. [f] Sew on the canvas base. [g] The loose cover tied on with tapes

CANVAS CHAIRS

Deck-chair

For re-covering an old deck-chair you will need canvas to replace the old material, some 10mm tacks, a hammer and a screwdriver. With the aid of the screwdriver, gouge out the old tacks. Buy new canvas to the same length, remembering to take the turnings into account.

At each end, fold under 2.5cm to the wrong side and press it in place. Lay the fabric right side down on the floor and sort the deck-chair out on top so that it too is facing downwards.

Bring the top end of the canvas round the top bar and hammer in a tack at the middle point. Be sure that it is straight and taut before hammering in further tacks at each end of the bar, and then more to fill in the gaps. Aim to fix a tack every 5 or 6cm.

Repeat the exercise for the bottom bar. This bar is slightly narrower so you will have to fold the canvas under at each side by about 2cm [**4.43**].

4.43 Deck-chair

4.44 Director's chair

100

Director's chair

Cut away the old canvas from the frame using a Stanley knife. Then cut round the canvas as near as possible to the nails, but don't try to gouge out the nails themselves or you may split the wood. Instead, hammer them flush with or into the surface of the wood.

Measure for the seat material before you ease the back off the uprights – otherwise the chair will collapse, making measuring difficult. Measure across from the outside of one side bar to the equivalent place on the other bar, and add about 5cm to the length. Use the old canvas as a pattern, adding 4cm for hems front and back. Likewise, use the back of the chair as a guide, adding on 5cm for turning under at the sides. Add 3cm to the depth.

When you cut out the fabric, see that the top of the back uses a selvedge. If using striped canvas be particularly careful that you cut both pieces quite straight.

Deal with the back first. Turn under and press the selvedge by 1cm. On the opposite sides, turn under a double 1cm hem. Machine-stitch along both these hems. Turn under and press 1cm at both short ends. Then, using the chair uprights as guides, pin the fold to the back of the fabric to form casings [4.44]. Machine the casings.

Give the seat double 1cm hems turned under along the front and back edges. Press under 2.5cm at each side, then collapse the chair and hammer in tacks through the hem every 5 or 6cm on the underside of the bar, being careful to avoid the old tacks. Finish the other side in the same way.

COVER FOR AN OTTOMAN

Many a household has a lidded box useful for storing linen and for sitting on. Unless it is a beautiful antique it may well benefit from being covered in fabric.

Check first that the structure is sound and that the hinges are in working order. You will need enough fabric to cover the top and the four sides – allow extra for centring any motifs [**4.45a**]. The fabric will hang next to the wood so if you want to achieve a softer look you could use quilted material. Buy enough lining fabric to fit the bottom and sides of the box, and for the underside of the lid if you don't want to use black upholstery lining there.

You will also need enough foam (1.5cm thick) and strong cardboard to line the bottom and sides of the box; upholstery tacks, a hammer, glue, and braid to go round the inner top edge of the box and round the lid. If you are giving a flat box a buttoned top you will also need chipboard the same size as the lid, a drill, broad-headed tacks, a long upholstery needle and strong thread, and, for deep-buttoning, a couple of kitchen spoons.

4.45a, b, c, d, e and f Ottoman: [a] Measure the basic box. [b] Cut outer panels. [c] Cut inner panels. [d] Fit the inner panels by tacking, or [e] sewing together a separate insert. [f] Finish the inside top edge with braid

First, cut the fabric into four outer panels for the front, back and sides of the box, with 2.5cm seam allowances where the panels will meet at the corners, and a 2.5cm allowance along the bottom edges. At the top, allow enough extra fabric to turn under the top edges and fix inside, plus a 2.5cm hem allowance [4.45b].

For the inside of the box use a standard curtain lining fabric. The appearance of the lining will be improved if it is lightly padded with foam-covered board. For this, cut a rectangle of strong cardboard or thin hardboard to fit the bottom of the box. Glue to it a rectangle of 1.5cm thick foam of the same size. Cut a piece of lining fabric to the same size, with 2.5cm allowances all round, and stretch it over the foam-covered board. Glue the turnings to the board, mitring the corners [4.45c].

Cut four further pieces of board, foam and lining fabric to fit the inner sides of the box, and cover them similarly. You can either fit them individually or sew them all together. To fit them individually, push a tack through the covered panel near each corner. Hammer it home using a block to prevent the hammer damaging the fabric [4.45d]. To fit the lining panels together, hand-sew the edges to form a box-like structure and lower it into the ottoman [4.45e].

Sew the outer panels into one continuous band of fabric, right sides together. Slide the lining into the box and adjust it to fit at the corners. Mitre and slip stitch the fabric over the top edges of the box sides; turn the raw edges under where the outside fabric meets the lining, and slip stitch the two together all round. A simple length of braid sewn round the inside top edge will give a neat finish and conceal the join [4.45f]. Turn the bottom edge under, and hammer in tacks all round the base of the ottoman.

The cover for the lid may have a similar panel of padded lining underneath, with a top outer cover slip stitched to it. If the box or ottoman lid is fairly deep, trim and sew the corners of the top cover to fit. Press under the allowances of the lining and slip stitch it down over the raw edges of the top cover. The fabric needs to be trimmed and turned under round the hinges. A length of braid slip stitched round the edge of the lid gives a good finish.

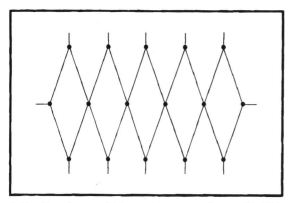

4.46   Experiment with buttoning patterns for a padded lid

4.47a and b   Buttoned lid: [a] Attach the button via a hole drilled in the board. [b] Use spoon handles to smooth out the pleats

For any flat-topped ottoman, a panel of 5cm foam fixed in place with a few spots of glue turns it into a convenient seat. If you are making up a box of your own, you can improve its appearance with a simple pattern of buttoning.

Start by drawing a pattern of button points, and sketch in the pleats between them [**4.46**]. An upholstery materials supplier will provide you with buttons and may also cover them for you if you take along a length of the fabric; or you can buy buttons from any large haberdashery department and cover them yourself.

At the points where the buttons will fit, drill holes through the chipboard. Next to each hole hammer halfway home on the underside a short broad-headed upholstery tack. Glue the foam in place and lay the covering fabric loosely over it. Hammer in a couple of tacks or drawing-pins to hold the fabric while you work.

Starting at the centre buttonhole, sew up from the back of the hole through the board, the foam and the top cover. Use a good strong upholstery thread, because the buttons will be subjected to considerable strain. Thread the loop of the button on to the thread, and take the needle back down through the fabric and the foam, using a slightly different path. Return through the hole in the board, pull the thread taut, and tie the ends firmly round the tack next to the hole [**4.47a**].

Move on to the next hole and sew up through it and the foam. Draw the fabric firmly into place, press it down over the needle, draw the needle through, thread on the button, and return the thread through the fabric and foam. Pull the thread taut and secure it round the tack. When you are confident that you have got the set of the fabric right and will not have to rework the button, hammer home both tacks.

If you are using very thick foam, the fabric will need pleating between the button points, and the effect will be deep-buttoning. To shape the pleats you need a couple of spoons. Using the handles, tuck one under the pleat between the two buttons and hold the other over the pleat. Slide them gently along the fabric in the same direction to form a neat and tidy pleat [**4.47b**].

Go on to a third buttonhole. Sew and secure the button, and tidy up the pleat as you go. As the pattern spreads you will have more than one pleat at some buttons. Remember to tidy the pleats before you proceed too far or the pleat will become inaccessible.

When you have completed the pattern, turn the fabric over the edges of the board and mitre the corners. Apply your lining, turning under and hand-sewing the edges. Ordinary lining fabric is acceptable for the job, but you will achieve a much smarter finish with stiff black upholstery lining. Fold it to the right dimensions to lie neatly within the edges of the board, and secure it with small, broad-headed upholstery tacks at intervals of about 2.5cm.

5   Lampshades

Making lampshades is one of the most rewarding activities in soft furnishing, especially from the creative and financial points of view. If you have the patience, you can produce exquisite shades to almost any design you like. The work is delicate and small in scale but vitally important to any decorating scheme. If you get the lighting right, a room will look at its best; if the lighting is wrong, even the most expensive and elegant furnishings can look dead and uninviting. In terms of money, the savings in this area are perhaps greater than in any other area of soft furnishing: the lampshade takes so little material that you can make it at little cost, using left-over pieces of fabric.

The range of lampshade shapes is extensive, and choice of fabric to cover them almost infinite. It is best to acquire some experience by making a simple shade first so that you learn what effects can be achieved. Experiment with scraps of material held in front of a naked bulb, bearing in mind the purpose of the lamp. If it is a reading lamp, avoid dark colours unless the shape of the frame allows a wide diffusion of light at the bottom. Whites and reds shed a rather harsh light (though white can be warmed up with a coloured lining), and blues a cool one. Popular colours are various shades of pink, apricot, yellow and cream, all of which create a warm effect.

Plain designs are usually the most effective as well as the most efficient. In any case, the light will show up any structural defects which are more likely to occur with a complicated design.

The fabric should be washable and strong enough to be stretched on to the frame, but not too thick. For these reasons crêpe-backed satin, silk shantung and wild silk are extravagant but very good choices for a tailored lampshade. Taffeta and lining fabrics wear too easily and show pin marks. Gathered tiffany lampshades look good in dress cottons, lawn and gingham or, for a still more delicate effect, in lined broderie anglaise and lace. If you are making a pleated shade you will need silk chiffon or some other soft fabric that drapes well.

For firm lampshades (see page 119) milliner's buckram on its own makes an effective home-spun-looking shade, or can be used to stiffen paper, lace or other soft fabric.

Whichever fabric you choose, make sure that it is not easily flammable – remember that it will be close to a hot light bulb. Make it clear to the sales assistant that the fabric is for a lampshade lining. Flame-proof linings are obtainable and, although crêpe is the best, cotton lawn and fine lawn are also suitable.

THE BASIC SHADE

Tools and materials for fabric lampshades
The basis of any lampshade is the frame, obtainable in the furnishing department of most stores and at many small shops that specialise in household furnishings. The frame is a strong structure in copper or steel wire with, typically, a ring at the top and bottom, and several upright struts, all welded together. In the middle is a lampholder, often an adjustable gimbal so that the shade will tilt to throw light at a particular angle.

Choose the frame in conjunction with the base of the lamp before you make the shade – otherwise the proportions may emerge unbalanced. Check that it has the correct fitting for a standard or floor lamp, a table lamp, clip-on or pendant lamp. Soft fabric shades will need a strutted frame as well as rings top and bottom, while firm shades need only a ring set with the appropriate fitting (a strutted frame can be used but is not essential). Large frames can be difficult for a beginner to handle, so pick a small one of relatively straightforward shape. Avoid the small 'candle-shade' frames – they are the most difficult to handle.

You may want to resurrect an old frame – see *Binding the frame* for the way to prepare it.

You will also need binding tape. Standard white tape about 1–1.5cm wide is fine if you can't buy unbleached loose-woven lampshade tape.

Tiffany shade

Square shade

Straight-sided drum

Tapered drum

Pendant tiffany shade

Sectional shade

Butterfly clip for small shades

Ring set for firm shades

Gimbal rings

5.1   A range of lampshade frames

Buy 2½ times the total length of the circumference of the rings and the length of all the struts. (You will not need to bind the bulb fitting.) Buy also a cold-water dye to tint the bound frame the same colour as the main fabric. You could use bias binding bought to match – if so, iron out one of the creased edges before using it.

Small fine-gauge pins are essential, no longer than 2.5cm (smaller than some dressmaking pins). Other necessary pieces of equipment are 'sharps' needles (grades 3–9) for fabric lampshades, and 'betweens' needles (5–6) for firm shades; a fabric tape measure; dressmaking scissors (nail scissors are also useful); adhesive for fixing trimmings; a metal file or fine sandpaper; and quick-drying enamel paint or plastic varnish if you are using an old frame. You will also need lengths of string and 7.5mm elastic for a gathered tiffany shade.

Finally, you will probably want to trim the top and bottom edges of the shade with a braid or fringe.

There is a huge variety to choose from but again, the simpler ones tend to be the most effective, perhaps a plain braid about 5–10mm wide in a colour which tones with the main fabric.

106

5.2a, b and c Binding a lampshade: [a] Start at the top of the frame. [b] Binding pattern and procedure. [c] To turn at a corner

Binding the frame

There are two schools of thought on how to prepare a frame. Some lampshade-makers prefer to bind tape round the entire metal part to prevent the hard profile showing through the fabric. Others find this unnecessary. Many frames are already coated in white plastic or enamel when you buy them, and the full binding then becomes superfluous. Even so, you will have to bind the top and bottom rings and the vertical struts at two opposite sides to give you a base to pin the fabric to.

The best plan is to bind your first frame all round. You can then decide whether you would prefer to use partially bound frames on later projects.

First, take a file or sandpaper to the frame and file down any sharp corners – just enough to round off the hard edge. On an old frame, sandpaper off any rust and paint the frame with plastic varnish or enamel paint. This is especially important if you ever intend to wash the shade. On a new shade with plastic coating, shave off any lumps of excess plastic, particularly round the joints. Make sure that movable parts on a gimbal fitting are free-moving, and correct any misalignments in the frame by gently bending the metal.

Measure along the top of the frame between

two struts, down one of them and along the bottom of the frame between the two uprights. Multiply this length by 2½, and cut off that much tape from your roll. Start at the inside top of the frame where a strut meets the top ring, with the tape held against the inside of the frame. Pull the tape out over the frame and down through the centre, to secure the end [**5.2a**]. Make a few turns along the ring, sloping each one away from the starting point at an acute angle and keeping the tape taut. Some people wind the tape round a small card but you will probably find it easier to throw the loose end over and pull it through.

One problem which you will soon encounter is that the tape tends to gape at the overlaps. You must make the elasticity of the tape work to eliminate this gaping as much as you can, stretching and pulling the tape to make it lie flat against the previous turn. Make the binding as neat and flat as possible, and avoid double overlaps which will produce too much bulk.

You will arrive at the first upright strut: the binding must go down that strut, then along the bottom ring, to form a Z-shape [**5.2b**].

To turn the corner, simply bind one turn beyond the strut, then reverse the binding, take the tape behind the upright, and start winding down the upright itself so that you effect a figure of eight [**5.2c**].

Bind down the upright, turn the corner, and go along to the next corner. If your original measuring was accurate and your binding has been neat, you should end up with just the right amount to reach that corner. If you have too much, go back and check that you have no serious gaps, and rework the length. If it falls short, you will almost certainly have used insufficient pull along the frame, resulting in too much bulk. You will probably find small gaps at the corners, where the frame shows through. This doesn't matter as they will be covered later by other lengths of tape.

When you come to the end of the first length, pin the tape to itself and cut a new length. Start it at the top of the frame to meet the first length of binding, and follow the same Z-shape. At the bottom of the second upright you will encounter the end of the first length of tape. Take out the pin and bind the second tape round the first as you did at the previous corner. Each length of tape will secure the length before it. Eventually you will come to the bottom of your first upright strut. Pin that last length in place, then sew it for a firm fixing, making the stitches on the outside of the frame – these will be hidden by the outer fabric. The cover of the shade will itself fix the binding in place all round. The binding should be quite taut and firm so that the cover will not slip.

Now dye the bound frame to the required colour of the main fabric or lining, using a cold-water dye.

The cover

Let us presume that you have an 'empire' frame which is wider at the bottom than at the top and which has six panels. Many shades are made to this pattern. Take the measurement of three panels round the bottom of the frame. Measure the height of the frame. Add a generous 10cm to both measurements. This should be enough to cater for any curve in the upright struts. If the curve is pronounced and the shade a large one, add a little more to make sure you buy enough material. You can now cut a rectangle to cover three panels (half) of the frame.

The selvedge or straight grain of the material should run from top to bottom, unless the shape of the frame is waisted. If that is the case, gain greater flexibility by cutting the material on the bias where the grain of the fabric runs diagonally to the sides of the rectangle.

Now, spread the fabric over the frame to cover the three panels as accurately as you can. The fabric must overhang the frame on all sides. Insert a pin through the fabric and the binding at the four corners [5.3a]. Draw the fabric fairly taut, and pin it to the binding with three more pins each at top and bottom. Pins along the top and bottom rings should face into the middle, and those down the sides should face outwards. This is to reduce damage to both you and the shade. (If you do prick your finger and get blood on the fabric, moisten some tacking cotton and dab it at once on to the bloodstain.)

Pin the fabric in place to the two uprights. Unpin the top, ease and draw up the fabric and pin it again. That may throw the fabric out of true between the top and bottom rings so unpin it at one or the other, smooth any wrinkles and re-pin it. Continue like this until you achieve a straight, crease-free covering over that half of the frame, without stretching the fabric [**5.3b**]. The pins will be at intervals of about 5mm. If you have done the job badly, take off the fabric, straighten the frame and start again.

When you are satisfied, trim off the surplus fabric to 2.5cm from the frame all round. Mark the position of the frame. Dressmaker's chalk is best but you could use a pencil lightly. Rub it over the fabric along the line of the frame all round, then take out all the pins. Mark the centre panel with a pin through the binding. It pays to return the fabric on to exactly the same area when you re-fit it.

Lay the fabric flat and trim it more accurately, with a 1.5cm border round the chalk mark. Next cut the fabric for the opposite side of the frame.

Lay the first piece on the cutting length for the second piece, wrong side to wrong side. Pin them together all round so that they do not move, and cut the second piece to exactly the same size as the first. Alternatively, you could pin a double layer of fabric to the shade from the start. Make sure that the two layers are mirror images of each other by placing their wrong sides together. You can only do this if the fabric is fairly fine.

5.3a and b Fitting the cover fabric: [a] Pin through the fabric and frame binding at four corners. [b] Then fill in the gaps

109

5.4a and b Fitting the lining fabric: [a] Pin along the lower edge. [b] Fit the fabric round the lamp fitting at the top

The lining

Balloon lining is a standard lining fixed top and bottom to the frame. Fold the lining fabric in half, wrong sides together so that the straight grain of the fabric will run from top to bottom of the shade. Lay the pinned outer fabric on top of it. Cut the doubled lining to exactly the same size.

Return to the outer panels and re-pin them along the marked line; then machine-sew them together, right side to right side, along the chalked or pencilled guideline. Stretch the fabric slightly as you go – this will prevent the stitches breaking later when the cover is pulled over the frame. Sew the lining into a similar tube, but a fraction smaller than the outer fabric, and mark with chalk or pencil the top and bottom of the frame.

Trim off the excess on the two parts of the outer cover and lining, to 5mm from the seams only, not at the top and bottom. Then press the cover flat but do not open the seams. The cover is now ready for fitting.

Start with the lining. Open it out inside the frame, wrong side towards the frame, and make sure that the seams coincide with those struts where the seams in the outer fabric will eventually fall. Line up the horizontal chalk or pencil marks with the top and bottom of the frame [**5.4a**].

Turn the excess over the bottom ring and put in a few pins on the outside edge to hold it in place. Invert the frame, and ease the lining through tidily to the smaller top ring. Do not draw it too tight. At the sides, where the lampholder is welded on, unpick the seam just enough to allow you to bring the fabric up round the junction of the frame and gimbal or lampholder. Turn under the raw edges round the cut, and fold the excess fabric over to the outside of the ring [**5.4b**]. Do not pull it too hard or you will force the lower fabric out of place. Stick a few pins into the binding. Then start shaping the lining by taking out a few pins, tightening it gradually top and bottom, and re-pinning. Go right round, aiming to get a good set to the fabric. Be prepared to work at it, pulling out any unevenness and eliminating any wrinkles.

When you are satisfied, oversew it to the binding all round with very small stitches. Your sewing lines should be on the outside edges of the rings [**5.5a**]. Later those areas will be covered.

Cut two new rectangles of the lining fabric, each 10cm by 4cm. Fold each one into three along its length and thread them under the struts of the lampholder, one on each side. Turn them over to the outside of the frame, pin them in place and sew them, again on the outside edge of the top ring. They conceal the gap which you made to fit the lining fabric up into the angle of the gimbal or lampholder. Trim the lining fabric close to the sewing line [**5.5b**].

Fitting the cover
Now slide on the outer cover. Adjust it so that the panels lie where you originally fitted them. The seams of the outer cover and lining should match. Pin the fabric in place, top and bottom, starting at the two seam struts.

The outer cover fabric should be a perfect fit, but again you will have to ease it into place, removing any puckering. You can improve the finished product by leaving the lampshade unfinished for a couple of days. Fit the outer cover and put the shade in the room where it will be used. It will absorb atmospheric moisture, and you may see some slackness appear. You can take this up before finally sewing it in place.

Sew the cover to the top and bottom rings of the frame along the same sewing line as the lining, that is, on the outside edge of the frame. Use small stitches, and be careful not to let the sewing line creep over on to the crest of the binding. Trim the fabric as close to the sewing line as possible. This can be done most easily with sharp nail scissors.

5.5a and b Sewing the lining: [**a**] Oversew to the binding. [**b**] Conceal the gaps with strips of fabric and trim the lining close to the sewing line

111

Finishing

Almost any kind of braid or ruche will do the job, or elasticated ribbon, any of them in either a matching or a contrasting colour. You could instead make a trim yourself, the simplest version being 'self-trim'. Cut two strips of the cover fabric, each 3cm wide, one long enough to go round the top ring, the other to fit the bottom ring. They should be cut on the bias for flexibility if you have enough spare fabric. Fold each one into three along its length, like bias binding, and press it.

5.6 Sew on the trimming

Measure the circumference of each ring and add a good 5cm to each length to allow for turnings. Never stretch a trim to fit the frame as it will distort the cover. For this reason be particularly careful when applying elasticated ribbon. Fold under 1cm at the end of the trimming and, starting at one strut, pin it on just ahead of your ladder stitching. Keep the stitches as small as possible and do not let them stray into the inside of the shade [5.6]. When you have pinned and sewn all round the ring, cut the trimming exactly so that there is 1cm extra for turning under, and abut it with the beginning by slip stitching the ends together. The joins in the trimming at top and bottom should occur at the same strut.

Velvet ribbon is best glued to the shade since stitching would spoil it, and the fabric lacks the elasticity required for sewing. Glueing is a perfectly feasible alternative for other trims, too. Apply a thin layer of clear-drying glue to about 15cm only of the trimming, line it up neatly with the top or bottom of the frame, and press the surfaces together for a short while. Continue glueing round each ring, abutting the turned-under ends as before. Peg the ends together until they have dried thoroughly.

SQUARE SHADE

The square shade looks relatively simple but requires as much skill in pulling the fabric into shape as for the round type. A distorted panel of fabric will seriously mar its appearance.

Start by binding the frame as before. Then cut four panels of fabric, all of them on the straight grain. Measure the dimensions and add about 5cm to the height and width of each panel.

Cut the lining to the same dimensions as the outer fabric. Balloon lining is not suitable for this type of frame and the outer fabric and lining should be fitted together as a single layer. Machine-sew them wrong sides together, 2cm from the edge and certainly within the area that will be excess when each panel is fitted to the frame.

Pin each one to the binding as on the earlier version, and pull and stretch the fabric to a comfortable, taut fit. Start pinning at the centre bottom and pull to the centre top. Draw and ease the fabric down to the two bottom corners in turn, then towards the two top corners. Put in plenty of pins, and be prepared to take them out and re-pin to achieve a good set to the fabric. Finally, pull the fabric across to the sides. See [5.7] for the order in which to ease the fabric.

Sew each panel to the binding with the usual small stitches, exactly on the crest of the frame. Trim away the excess fabric as close to the new sewing line as you comfortably can without cutting into it.

Complete all four panels. You must now add a trim to the four long edges to conceal the sewing line. Self-trim is good for this purpose, or you could use a braid. You will need four pieces, each long enough for one of the upright struts. First, secure the bottom end by sewing it to the binding on the frame. Apply glue in short sections to fix the outer edges of the trim to the cover fabric, or sew the pieces securely to the top of the frame. Do not pull the trim too tight.

Finally, trim the top and bottom of the frame as on the previous shade. Self-trim or any manufactured braid will do.

This is the best method for all large lampshades where to handle more than one panel at a time would be unwieldy.

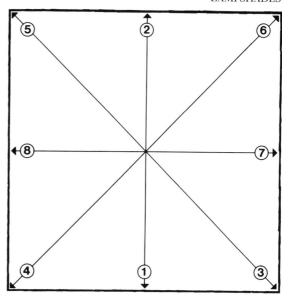

5.7 The order in which to ease the fabric over the panels of a square-sided frame

5.8   Constructing a pleated shade

PLEATED SHADES

Among the more elaborate shades, perhaps especially appropriate for bedroom lighting, are shades with pleated covers. Chiffon is particularly recommended but georgette is also suitable. Nylon does not pleat well. This type of shade gives a soft appearance and diffuses light well. Use either a straight-sided drum or a tapered frame. The outer cover will be fitted to give a loosely pleated finish but the lining is fitted smooth.

Bind the frame as before. To fit the lining, measure the frame's circumference and height, and cut the lining to the approximate size of four workable panels. Pin it all round the inside of the bottom of the frame. Arrange the joins to fall at the upright struts, and turn the fabric out towards you as you sew it to the binding so that the cover will later conceal the raw edges. You will have to unpick the seams just enough to pass the lampholder struts, as before.

Cut the chiffon for the outer cover, approximately three times as long as the circumference of the bottom ring, and a good 10cm wider than the depth of the shade. Cut across the fabric so that the straight grain will run from top to bottom down the shade. Don't worry if you haven't a complete length of material, but see below for dealing with joins.

Start at one of the struts and turn under 5mm along the raw edge. Pin the material to the bottom binding, gathering it into tiny pleats as you go, approximately 1–2cm all round the frame. This will be easier on a straight drum frame; on a tapered frame the main difficulty lies in keeping the pleats straight up to the top ring. Use the struts as a guide and work in a symmetrical pattern, vertical at the centres sloping to the sides at the struts, and merging neatly between the two. There must be the same number of pleats between each strut. Join the fabric at the same strut

114

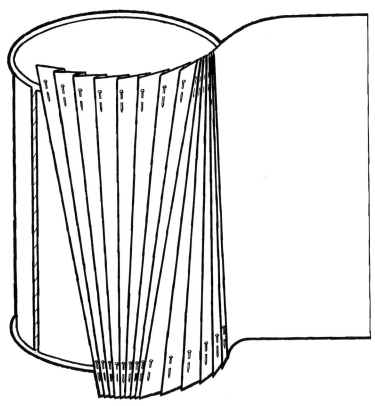

5.9   Fan pleating

as the lining, again by turning it under, and slipping the other raw edge behind it [5.8]. When the material is pleated satisfactorily top and bottom, sew the fabric to the binding.

If you have to work the shade for more than one length of material, do not sew down the join but merely turn under the new length and position it over the previous raw edge to form the next pleat. When you get back to the beginning, trim the raw edge to the correct length and tuck it under the fold of the first pleat. Trim close to the stitching before finishing the shade with a suitable braid or fringe as before.

An attractive variation is to pleat round the top ring but gather along the bottom edge. Adjust the gathers evenly before you sew. Another possibility is to plan small gaps between the pleats; or you could tackle fan pleating (only possible on a straight-side frame) by arranging equal alternate sections of pleating [5.9].

HANDKERCHIEF SHADE

An extremely simple design for a lampshade is the handkerchief lampshade. You will need a utility ring and a square metre of fabric. Cotton or lawn would be a good choice of fabric. Sew round the square in a double hem turned to the wrong side, or make a scalloped edge with machine-zigzagging, and trim the edge after sewing. Use sharp nail scissors for the job.

Fold the fabric in four to find the centre, mark it, and cut a hole just large enough for the flex from the ceiling to pass through it. Bind the hole by hand-overcasting or machine-zigzagging, or use bias binding.

Feed the flex through the hole, connect the utility ring, the lightbulb holder and the bulb.

115

TIFFANY SHADES

These lampshades are popular for many rooms
and range from an informal and pretty style in
such fabrics as gingham, lawn, lace or broderie
anglaise, through to a more tailored and luxurious look, perhaps for a formal table lamp, in a
heavy silk.

There are two construction methods – the
gathered tube and the tailored version. The gathered tube is easier and more informal and can
have a frill round the bottom edge. Start by preparing and binding the frame as usual. For the
gathered style you need only bind the rings, but
the tailored version should be bound on every
third strut, dividing the frame into quarters.

5.10a, b and c Tiffany shade: [a] Construct the cover
and lining. [b] Mark the position of a lower frill on the
frame. [c] Sew the frill to the fitting line

116

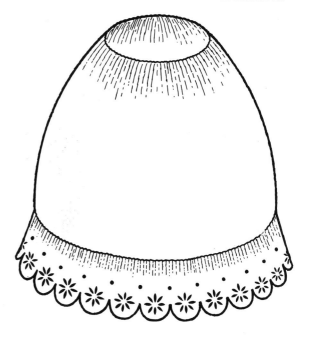

The gathered version Measure round the circumference of the bottom ring and add 10cm. The width of the material will be the depth of the frame plus about 6cm. The fabric must be cut so that the straight grain will run down the shade from the top to bottom. If you haven't enough material to cut the piece from a single length, make it up from two equal lengths, so that the seam will fall exactly at a strut.

You will need the same amount of lining fabric. Treat the top and lining fabrics as one by joining them wrong sides together with a French seam (so start with the fabrics right sides out). Press the finished seam to one side.

At both long edges turn in a double 1.25cm casing. Leave a 3 or 4cm gap at the seams for inserting elastic [**5.10a**]. Introduce lengths of string into each casing and try the shade on the frame, adjusting each piece to fit. These will be the lengths of the elastic needed, but add on a centimetre or so to secure the ends.

If you are planning to have a frill at the bottom edge, mark the position of its sewing line while it is on the frame. This will be along the edge of the bottom ring [**5.10b**].

Insert elastic into both casings, secure the ends, and close the gaps in the casings by hemming.

The frill should also be cut on the straight grain. It should be 10–15cm wide and 1½ times the length of the circumference of the bottom ring. Join the two short ends in a narrow French seam. Fold the material in two lengthwise, right sides out. Turn under the raw edges just over 1cm at the top. Gather within that margin through the layers. Draw up the gathers evenly, pin the frill to the fitting line and sew it neatly to the cover [**5.10c**].

Tailored tiffany shade

The work involved in making a tailored tiffany shade is much more like that for the standard shade, except that it is made in four sections, each one covering three panels.

Both the lining and the top material should be cut on the bias in order to get a better fit. You may find it easiest to make a paper pattern which you can then arrange on the fabric in order to find out how much to buy. Remember to allow more for matching up strongly patterned fabrics.

The lining first. It is fitted to the outside of the frame. Pin it to the outer strut and along the rings, easing and adjusting as usual. Trim the excess material to 1.5cm at the struts and 2.5cm at top and bottom. Oversew the lining to the binding along all the edges. Then trim one side, probably the right-hand one, close to the strut [5.11a]. Start fitting the next panel at this trimmed edge.

When you have lined the shade, deal with the main cover in the same way, but trim the excess fabric close to the rings as well as the struts. Cut slits in the lining down to the top ring so that it can turn over the top. Sew low down round the ring, and trim the surplus [5.11b and c]. Repeat for the bottom ring.

Glue self-trim or other suitable braid down the seamed struts in order to cover the stitching, as explained on page 112. Also attach some of the trim round the top ring by stab-stitching over and under the ring [5.11d], abutting the ends. Glue fringing or braid round the bottom ring.

5.11a, b, c and d   Tailored tiffany shade: [a] Oversew each panel to the binding. [b] Fit the main fabric, cut slits in the lining, turn down and sew. [c] Trim away the surplus fabric. [d] Attach the trimming

FIRM SHADES

The principles involved in making firm lamp-shades are not greatly different from those applied to soft fabric shades, but paper covers offer a greater scope for creative variations, such as attaching pressed dried flowers or appliqué work, painting the panels, and so on.

As well as the usual equipment for the other type of lampshade-making, you will need a ring set – two rings for the top and bottom of the shade, one attached to the appropriate lamp-holder fitting whether gimbal or pendant – a metal ruler, clear-setting glue and hinged woo-den clothes pegs. A strutted frame can also be used for a base.

Firm lampshades do not need lining. The choice of material used for the cover is not wide: real parchment is the traditional material but buckram is more usual and very much cheaper. Buckram, particularly the rough-textured type used for pelmets, can stand effectively on its own, be painted, or be used as a backing for a softer fabric such as cotton, lace or even embroidered panels. Hand-painting on a panel of pale buck-ram would show off an additional accomplish-ment. A limited range of lampshade parchments with fabric already attached is available in large stores, and covered lampshade card too. For the rest of this chapter we will refer only to buckram.

The easiest shape to deal with is a straight-sided drum. The rings in the set should be the same size as each other. You need buckram the height of the finished shade (plus about 5cm) by the circumference of the rings (plus 2cm or so). It is wise to make a paper pattern so that you can assess the proportions – any fabric cover for the buckram can also be cut from it. The pattern must be cut with the corners square.

Bind each ring as usual. If you are covering a strutted frame you don't need to bind the struts. If you are attaching fabric to the buckram, do so before you cut out the rectangle. Wipe over its smooth side with a damp sponge before pressing on the fabric (right side out) with a hot iron. Cover the fabric with a damp cloth and iron the bonded material again.

119

5.12a and b Firm drum shade: [a] Peg the paper to the glued rings. [b] Stitch the paper to the binding with either straight or blanket stitch

5.13 Make a paper pattern for a conical strutted frame by rolling the shade and marking the dimensions

There are two methods for attaching the buckram to the shade. The first is to apply a thin layer of glue round the outside of one of the rings. Peg the cover to it so that the edge of the paper extends beyond the ring by a bare 5mm. Leave the excess for the overlapped seam down the side unglued. Treat the other ring in the same way. Adjust the side seam allowance by trimming it to an exact 5mm, and glue the join [**5.12a**]. When the glue has dried, stitch along the top and bottom to attach the cover to the binding. Use double thread, and make small stitches inside the drum [**5.12b**]. You can make them slightly longer on the outside where they will be covered by braid. Glueing on the braid or other trimming is the final stage of the construction. The abutted ends top and bottom should be at the same side of the frame.

The other method dispenses with glue except for the side seam and for attaching the trim. The top and bottom edges of the shade must be trimmed flush to the outer edges of the rings. Blanket-stitch through the buckram round the rings, stopping short of the side seam by 5cm. Mark with a light pencil on the wrong side of the buckram the exact vertical to form a neat overlap. Glue it down and resume the blanket-stitching to close the gaps top and bottom. Glue the braid or trimming round the rings, covering the blanket-stitching.

A paper pattern is necessary for any other shape such as a cone or straight-sided empire shade.

Bind the rings or frame as usual. For a strutted frame, take a large piece of stiff paper. Mark down one of the side struts with pencil. Gradually turn the frame keeping it level, marking the curve formed by the two rings and also the position of each strut until you arrive back at the beginning. Add on 1.5cm for a seam allowance [**5.13**].

If the frame is very large, make a pattern of half of it, and cut two pieces from it, one the reverse of the other. Fit the pattern to the frame to make any adjustments before you cut out the buckram.

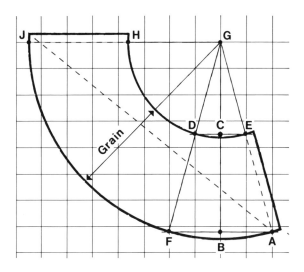

5.14 For a ring set, make a pattern using graph paper

For a ring set you will need some graph paper [**5.14**]. Measure the intended height of the shade and the diameter and circumference of each of the rings. From the corner of the graph paper at **A**, plot the diameter of the bottom ring to **F**. From the middle point of that line (**B**) take up a vertical, the height of the shade. Draw another horizontal line through that point (**C**) the length of the diameter of the top ring. Join the ends of the two horizontal lines which will give a shape resembling the frame itself (**FDEA**). Continue them until they meet. Use that junction (**G**) as a pivotal point: fix a pencil to a piece of string the exact length of **GE**. Fix the loose end of the string to **G** with a drawing-pin. Draw an arc from **E** round to **H**, the arc being the circumference of the top ring. Perform a similar operation with another piece of string the exact length of **GA**, taking the pencil round to **J**. That arc will be the circumference of the bottom ring.

You will now have the exact size of the shade (**JHEA**) but add 5mm to one edge to form an overlap. A line drawn through **JH** should arrive at **G** if you have plotted the measurements accurately. The grain line guide for the fabric will divide the wedge in two. Cut out the pattern and test it by pegging it on the rings. When you arrive at a satisfactory fit proceed as described for the drum shade.

Care of lampshades
If you plan to wash the lampshade, bear this in mind from the planning stages and choose colour fast fabric, lining and trimming. The shade must dry as quickly as possible to prevent the frame rusting. Use a mild detergent, rinse the shade thoroughly in warm water and dry it in the sun. A spell afterwards in an airing cupboard or other warm spot will help the fabric to tauten on the frame.

Firm shades and non-washable fabrics should be kept clean by regular soft brushing. Scotchguard produces an aerosol for protecting clothes which can also be sprayed on a finished lampshade to protect it from spots and stains.

6 Table linen

This section contains some of the quickest, easiest and least expensive projects in the book that also lend themselves to great adaptation and variation. For instance, you could make several tablecloths of different lengths and edgings for different occasions, with matching or contrasting mats and napkins.

Reversible quilting is particularly suitable for mats and tea cosies, and for the top of the round gathered tablecloth because of its insulating qualities. Polyester/cotton mixtures are good for cloths and napkins, and cotton seersucker needs little ironing. Some loose-weave materials are also appropriate for cloths but above all the fabrics used in this section should be washable, colourfast and easily ironed.

ROUND TABLECLOTH

Measure the table's diameter and the margin of overhang that you want. If you are making a floor-length tablecloth, allow for it just to clear the floor. To the table top's diameter, add on twice the height of the overhang, plus 6cm for two double 1.5cm hems.

With run-and-fell seams, join widths of fabric as necessary on each side of the main part in order to make up just over the approximate measurement you want. Fold the material in half, right sides together, so that the seams coincide, and fold in the other direction so that you get a rough square. Attach a piece of string to dressmaker's chalk or an ordinary pencil and pin the other end of the string through the corner where all the folds meet, such that the length of string is half the total diameter of the cloth [6.1]. Draw round the arc of the quarter-circle, and cut round the mark. Turn in a double 1.5cm hem and sew it with two rows of stitching. The first row will close the hem and you will have to ease the fullness in the fabric by snipping into the allowance. The second row should be close to the fold to define clearly the edge of tablecloth.

Fitted round tablecloth

A more complicated type of round tablecloth has a flat top with a gathered overhang usually descending right to the floor. Cut the top to the same surface area as the table allowing for a 1.5cm seam allowance all round. Lay it on the table and weight it so that it does not move. Then mark with pins all round the line of the table's edge. Sew piping round the seam if you wish.

The overhang is made in the form of a skirt, cut as a rectangle of cloth measuring up to twice the circumference of the circle.

The width will be the depth of the overhang plus 1.25cm for the seam at the top and 5cm for a double 2.5cm hem at the bottom. On a floor-length tablecloth the skirt should fall from the top of the table to the point just clearing the floor. Join the two ends of the skirt into a continuous circle. Turn up and hand-sew the double hem, checking that any pattern is upright.

Divide both the length of the skirt and the circumference of the circle into four equal parts, marking them with pins [6.2a]. Gather up the

6.1 How to make a circle for a round tablecloth

6.2a and b Fitted round tablecloth: [a] Divide the top circle and skirt into quarters. [b] Gather up each skirt quarter

skirt with two rows of thread about 5mm apart, working to the quarter-circumference measurement in order to gather an even skirt all round [**6.2b**]. Otherwise, it is easy to be left with too much fullness at one side and too little at the other.

Machine-sew the skirt to the top seam allowance (1.5cm) with at least two rows of stitching for strength.

Scalloped edging

If your sewing-machine has a zigzag facility, satin-stitching sewn in scallop shapes can give an attractive edge to a tablecloth, round or square. Measure and cut the fabric, and with dressmaker's chalk draw round the edge of a saucer or wineglass to form a series of arcs [**6.3**].

Zigzag stitch all round in a similar or contrasting colour. Trim off the excess cloth without cutting the thread – you may find nail scissors the best tool for the job. You could also follow shapes in the fabric itself to produce an irregular scalloped effect.

6.3 Make a scalloped edge by drawing arcs round a saucer or wineglass

123

6.4   Pull threads with a needle tip to form a fringe on fabric mats or napkins

TABLE MATS

You can set a table mat on a tablecloth or use it directly on the table as a protection for the furniture. Do not rely on anything other than quilted fabric or fabric backed with synthetic wadding to shield the table from hot plates. Whatever you use should be washable and colourfast.

Start with a rectangle of fabric about 23 × 30cm – this is a useful size because you can cut four pieces from a single width of 120cm fabric.

You could hand-sew a simple double hem all round or add a braid or bias edging. You could also sew a double line of stitches 1 or 2cm from each edge to fix the fabric, and with a needle carefully pull away the threads outside the stitches to form a fringe [**6.4**].

Or try the zigzag stitch on your sewing-machine, perhaps using an interesting colour for the thread to echo the scalloped edging on a tablecloth.

Patchwork, quilting (page 14), appliqué work and embroidery can all be brought into play in the making of attractive table mats.

TABLE NAPKINS

Table napkins are generally square – sides of 50cm will be generous. A narrow double 5mm hem in conjunction with mitred corners produces the neatest finish, but you could give the napkin a contrasting hem in the form of bias binding sewn over the raw edge of the main fabric, or follow the scalloped edge theme.

TEA COSY

The usual type of tea cosy consists of an inner and an outer cover with wadding between to give the necessary insulation.

Take two roughly semi-circular pieces of easily washable cotton for the inner lining and pin them to fit comfortably over the tea-pot's spout and handle. Try them on the tea-pot before you cut round the shape. There should be enough material for turning up a small bottom hem at a later stage. Right sides together, sew a seam round the pin line. Trim the seam. Lay the inner cover on the outer fabric. Cut two pieces for the outer cover, 1.5cm larger than the finished lining, with a 1.5cm seam allowance all round.

Before sewing the cover, prepare a length of piping to run the length of the seam. Also make a loop, if you want to hang up the tea cosy, in the same fabric as the piping casing. Cut a piece of fabric 15cm by 6cm. Fold in the two long sides, right sides out, and then fold the strip over again. Slip stitch the long edges together. Pin the loop halfway along the tea cosy, and with right sides together and enclosing the piping, sew the main seam.

Cut two sheets of terylene wadding for the insulating layer. Cut them slightly smaller than the lining and catch stitch the edges to its seam allowance. Slip the outer cover over the whole assembly and turn in the hems of both the inner and outer covers. Machine-stitch or slip stitch them together by hand. You could enclose the finished bottom edge with binding to match the piping.

As a variation, try the four-cornered tea cosy. Again, it is wise to pin first to get the right shape before you cut any fabric. The idea on this cover is to taper the corners of four squares of fabric to a point at the centre top.

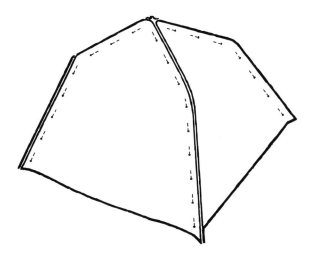

6.5 A tea cosy constructed from four panels

Pin the four pieces into a kind of tent [**6.5**]. When you have arrived at the best size and fit, use one piece as a template for the wadding, which should be very slightly smaller than the lining, and for the outer cover pieces – these should be larger than the lining by 1.5cm at each seam. Sew the lining pieces together and then the outer cover pieces, inserting the loop at the top and the piping down all the seams. Invert the outer cover only.

Catch stitch the nylon wadding to the seam allowances of the lining to hold it in place. Slip the outer cover over the lining. Machine-stitch or hand-sew round the bottom seam, or enclose it with binding to match the piping casing.

The simplest method of all is to use reversible quilted fabric cut to two semi-circles just larger than the tea-pot, and sewn together with or without piping or a hanging loop. Neaten the bottom edge with bias binding.

Suppliers

Many, even inexperienced needleworkers know of a local shop where they can buy the raw essentials for creating soft furnishings. Specialist shops are on the decrease but large stores have their own haberdashery departments that supply a range of materials, needlework equipment, headed tapes for curtainmaking, roller blind kits etc. Other sources for inexpensive materials include local charity and second-hand shops as well as the obvious standby – the jumble sale.

The ideas in this book can be complemented and expanded upon, to enable you to create very individual home furnishings – however you decide to experiment, the basics remain the same. Keep abreast of new ideas and fashions by buying home style magazines and picking up brochures from the major soft furnishings companies.

The following list of suppliers is not exhaustive and contains some of the major companies who will provide the raw materials. Contact their head office addresses for your local stockist.

Antique Textile Company
100 Portland Road
Holland Park
London W11 4LQ
071-221 7730

Laura Ashley Ltd
193 Warwick Road
London W14 8PU
071-603 2285
(0628) 39151 (*head office*)
(*and branches*)

Jane Churchill
135 Sloane Street
London SW1X 9AY
071-730 6379
and
81 Pimlico Road
London SW1W 8PH
071-730 8564

Colefax and Fowler
39 Brook Street
London W1Y 2JE
071-580 1066/
071-493 2231
(*and branches*)

Conran Shop
81 Fulham Road
London SW3 6RD
071-589 7401

Debenhams
1 Welbeck Street
London W1A 1DF
071-408 4444
(*and branches*)

Habitat
Hithercroft Road
Wallingford
Oxfordshire
OX10 9EU
(0491) 35000 (*head office*)
(*and branches*)

Charles Hammond Ltd
Chelsea Garden Market
Chelsea Harbour
Lots Road
London SW10 0XE
071-351 7281

Heals
196 Tottenham Court Road
London W1P 9LD
071-636 1666

Java Cotton Co
52 Lonsdale Road
London W11 5BY
071-229 3022

John Lewis
278–306 Oxford Street
London W1A 1EX
071-629 7711 (*head office*)
(*and branches*)

Liberty
214–220 Regent Street
London W1R 6AH
071-734 1234
(*and branches*)

Marks & Spencer
Michael House
47–67 Baker Street
London W1A 1DN
071-935 4422
(*and branches*)

Next Interiors
160 Regent Street
London W1R 5TA
071-434 2515
and
72 Kings Road
London SW3 4UG
071-584 1308
(0533) 866411 (*head office*)

Rufflette Ltd
Sharston Road
Wythenshawe
Manchester M22 4TH
061-998 1811

Arthur Sanderson & Son Ltd
52–53 Berners Street
London W1P 3AD
071-636 7800

Index

ACKNOWLEDGMENTS

Photographic credits for colour plate section
I Boys Syndication, Woodbridge, Suffolk; II (*top left and right*) Boys Syndication (*bottom left*) Jaycee Furniture Ltd, Brighton, East Sussex; III (*top left and right*) Boys Syndication (*bottom right*) Day Dreams Collection/Arthur Sanderson and Sons Ltd, London; IV Boys Syndication; V Boys Syndication; VI (*top left*) Boys Syndication (*bottom left*) Pallu & Lake (*bottom right*) Interior Selection, both of Coryton Destere Ltd, London; VII (*top left and right*) Interior Selection (*bottom*) Boys Syndication; VIII Boys Syndication; IX Boys Syndication; X Interior Selection; XI (*top*) Boys Syndication (*bottom left*) Pallu & Lake (*bottom right*) Boys Syndication; XII (*top*) Philip Dowell (*bottom*) Chatsworth Collection/Arthur Sanderson and Sons Ltd; XIII Fonthill Collection/Arthur Sanderson and Sons Ltd; XIV Boys Syndication; XV Boys Syndication; XVI Boys Syndication.

75p.